How to Work Remotely

CREATING SUCCESS
SERIES

The above titles are available from all good bookshops.

For further information on these and other Kogan Page titles, or to order online, visit the Kogan Page website at: www.koganpage.com.

How to Work Remotely

Work effectively, no matter where you are

Gemma Dale

KoganPage

Publisher's note
Every possible effort has been made to ensure that the information contained in this book is accurate at the time of going to press, and the publishers and author cannot accept responsibility for any errors or omissions, however caused. No responsibility for loss or damage occasioned to any person acting, or refraining from action, as a result of the material in this publication can be accepted by the editor, the publisher or the author.

First published in Great Britain and the United States in 2022 by Kogan Page Limited

2nd Floor, 45 Gee Street
London
EC1V 3RS
United Kingdom
www.koganpage.com

8 W 38th Street, Suite 902
New York, NY 10018
USA

4737/23 Ansari Road
Daryaganj
New Delhi 110002
India

Kogan Page books are printed on paper from sustainable forests.

ISBNs
Hardback   978 1 3986 0636 4
Paperback   978 1 3986 0611 1
Ebook   978 1 3986 0637 1

British Library Cataloguing-in-Publication Data
A CIP record for this book is available from the British Library.

Library of Congress Cataloging-in-Publication Data
Names: Dale, Gemma, author.
Title: How to work remotely : work effectively, no matter where you are / Gemma Dale.
Description: 1 Edition. | New York, NY : Kogan Page inc, [2022] | Includes bibliographical references.
Identifiers: LCCN 2022014702 (print) | LCCN 2022014703 (ebook) | ISBN 9781398606111 (paperback) | ISBN 9781398606364 (hardback) | ISBN 9781398606371 (ebook)
Subjects: LCSH: Telecommuting. | Flexible work arrangements. | Time management. | Employees–Rating of. | Organizational change.
Classification: LCC HD2336.3 .D373 2022 (print) | LCC HD2336.3 (ebook) | DDC 331.25/68–dc23/eng/20220506
LC record available at https://lccn.loc.gov/2022014702
LC ebook record available at https://lccn.loc.gov/2022014703

Typeset by Hong Kong FIVE Workshop
Print production managed by Jellyfish
Printed and bound by CPI Group (UK) Ltd, Croydon CR0 4YY

CONTENTS

01
An introduction to remote work

Remote work (also sometimes known as teleworking, virtual work, telecommuting or distributed work) refers to work that takes place outside of a traditional office environment. Many remote employees work from home, but remote working includes any form of work taking place away from a physical workplace and, typically, where colleagues are not co-located. It may include working in local hubs or co-working spaces too, or even working abroad or from a holiday home. Some remote teams meet occasionally, whereas others span countries and time zones and only ever connect virtually. Remote work takes place on a spectrum from fully remote work to a part-remote/part-office split, through to occasional or ad hoc home working while still being based predominantly in an office.

Remote working and home working are just two forms of flexible working; remote work can also be undertaken at the same time as other forms of flexibility such as time and schedule flexibility.

Remote work has only become truly possible as a result of technology – in particular the internet and affordable wifi. Technology has enabled us to truly work anywhere and any when. As early as the mid-1980s leading management thinkers were predicting that remote working would be the future of work. However, it took a global pandemic before many organizations took remote work seriously and introduced it at scale – largely as a necessity rather than through choice. Prior to the Covid-19 pandemic, those companies that were entirely remote were still few and far between.

Neither remote working nor home working are new ideas, but they escalated significantly as a result of Covid-19. It has been estimated that across Europe up to 100 million employees went to work from home in mid-2020, many of them doing so for the first time. In some countries up to half the working population spent an extensive period working from home, required to do so by their respective governments.

During this time, a strong, consistent and very global voice emerged – employees wanted to work from home more often in the future. Most of them, however, did not want to work remotely all of the time, but instead wanted to spend some of the time in offices with colleagues and some of the time working remotely. Both industry surveys and academic research (details of which you can find in the 'References and Further Reading' section of this book) typically found that around 60 to 80 per cent of employees wanted to work in this way. Organizations quickly responded, many of them confirming that employees would not be required to return to their offices – at least not all of the time. The idea of hybrid or blended working was born.

Although the pandemic drove this rapid shift to remote work, it has always been desired by employees, while not necessarily available to them. In 2019 the UK Chartered Institute of Personnel and Development described the progress of flexible working adoption as 'glacial', with many employees reporting that they could not access the type of flexible working they wanted or needed. Early research, however, now suggests that home working will stick after the Covid-19 pandemic. Organizations and individuals have both invested in home working; organizations in new technologies and training, and individuals in their own homes. Similarly, both organizations and their employees have found home working to be better than they might previously have believed possible. Jobs that were once considered unsuitable for remote working were proved to be so, and many managers realized that their fears that employees would misuse flexible or remote working were unfounded. In fact the majority of employees reported that they considered themselves to be at least as, if not more productive when working from home when compared to the office.

From an organizational point of view there are many potential benefits to introducing remote working. Research indicates that remote working, and indeed other forms of flexible working, can increase job satisfaction, reduce absenteeism, attract and retain talent and reduce estates costs (Dale, 2020). When people do work remotely, they usually tend to want to continue to do so, becoming strong advocates of it to others.

Together these factors point to a future that will be more flexible, and involve much more home or remote working than in the past. These new ways of working may take many forms. At one end of the spectrum remote work (or hybrid work) might simply mean working the occasional day from home; at the other end, 100 per cent remote work with no formal office base. For many though, the emerging expectation of hybrid and blended working (also sometimes referred to as 'part-remote') is that most people will spend a little time in each place each week depending on the type of work that they do. Organizations are likely to take a variety of different approaches depending on their own particular context, customers and stakeholders.

Of course, not every type of work can be undertaken remotely. It is largely the preserve of the knowledge worker – people whose work involves thinking, problem solving, writing or processing information. Whether a role is suitable for remote or home working will depend on several factors:

- the duties and responsibilities of the job itself
- operational requirements
- the needs of the team or organization
- the type of collaboration required with other people
- availability of enabling technology
- or the need for work to be completed at a specific place or time

Identifying the suitability of a role for remote working, and indeed whether an individual is able to undertake it effectively, are first steps in identifying potential for creating success.

Increased home and remote working has profound implications that stretch far beyond the workplace. It also means that those who will work remotely, and those who will lead remote teams, need to create the conditions for success in this new future. We are very familiar with how to operate and create career success in an office – we have after all been doing so since the Industrial Revolution. For many people, remote work before the pandemic was an occasional experience. As many learnt during the global pandemic, regular remote work is very different from working in the office as default, and hybrid working is different again.

Office work versus remote work

In an office, the working day is generally much more structured, especially in relation to time. Activities are typically synchronized with other employees. Colleague interactions mostly take place in person (unless we are sending emails from behind our closed office door which is all too often the case) and may be more ad hoc and casual – such as the often fabled 'watercooler conversation'. Office-based work is more inherently social than working remotely.

When working in person it can be easier to absorb organizational culture and build relationships. During the Covid-19 pandemic, employers estimated it was taking around a month longer to achieve an effective employee induction compared to in-person on-boarding. In contrast, working remotely can provide remote workers with more freedom around their working day; there is less need for strict start and end times (unless an employer demands them). The traditional commute is largely absent – potentially providing well-being and financial benefits. Communication is predominantly driven by technology and there can be fewer distractions than are often present in most offices, helping employees to improve their focus and productivity – especially those who find such environments challenging. It can, however, be more isolating as a result of those largely digital colleague connections, and some of that important social side of work can be lost through remote work. From a career point of view remote work can be less visible and employees therefore need to think differently about not just how to be successful but how to demonstrate it too.

Remote work versus hybrid work

Fully remote work and hybrid work also differ. Exactly how hybrid working takes place will vary from organization to organization, as well as from role to role. It does not necessarily follow therefore that someone who has successfully learnt to work in a hybrid way or remote way in one organization will be able to seamlessly transfer that experience to another. One of the most desired patterns of hybrid working is 3/2 – three days at home and two in the office – although in practice it takes many forms and involves many different levels of autonomy. Some employees will have total freedom to determine where they work and when, others will have fixed schedules or rotas. These issues present challenges for the hybrid worker – how to navigate the unique complexities of hybrid, especially when other employees remain co-located.

In some respects, hybrid work can deliver the best of both worlds; employees have the benefit of reduced commuting (a highly valued benefit) as well as time for focused and independent work. They also get regular face-to-face time with colleagues and the benefits that can bring to personal relationships and career success. Organizations can reap the financial benefits of requiring less office space, while supporting the well-being of staff and reducing facilities costs.

Hybrid work can, however, bring with it the challenges of both worlds too, both for hybrid workers and those who manage them. Hybrid work demands a diverse range of skills (as we will explore later in this chapter) as well as excellent organization. For those managing hybrid teams, excellent communication and collaboration skills are also required – they will need to work hard to make sure that everyone in the team has the information that they need in order to create team cohesion.

Neither working in person nor working remotely (or in a hybrid way) is necessarily 'better' than the other; outcomes will vary depending on personal working styles, organizational culture and the nature of the work itself.

Regardless of the specific type of remote work, it appears that new ways of working are here to stay – and therefore workers need to adapt too. The various forms of remote working requires a new skill set and a different approach. Some of what mattered in the office will matter more when working remotely. Some areas need a heightened focus whereas others become less important. Remote work has implications for well-being, inclusion, leadership and career development. This book will cover all of these areas, providing questions for reflection, tips for success and practical exercises to try. A personal and planned approach to remote working success is key. This book will help you to establish a plan that works for you.

The challenges of remote work – and how to overcome them

Working remotely has very real benefits to both workers and their organizations – but it comes with challenges too. The key to overcoming these challenges is to be aware of their potential and then have an appropriate strategy for ensuring that they don't derail career success. Some challenges, like well-being, we will explore in more detail later in this book. Other possible challenges include:

- effective collaboration with remote colleagues
- reduced contact with line manager for support and guidance
- building effective relationships

- career development and progression
- managing distractions and maintaining focus
- personal motivation
- isolation and loneliness
- starting a new role as a remote worker
- stigma associated with remote work

Of course, some of these challenges can exist in traditional working environments too. Each of these challenges will be explored throughout this book. The extent to which any of these amount to real business issues, and indeed how they should be addressed either for an individual or an organization, will depend on the specific circumstances.

Reflect

Which of these particular challenges are you most likely to experience based on your own particular circumstances, role or organization?

Hybrid work, the form of remote working that arose in response to the global pandemic, involves a blend of time in the office and time working remotely, usually from home. A particular challenge with hybrid working is its newness; we will only understand its impact and outcomes in the future when it is a firmly established and understood way of working. It will take time for good practice to emerge – as well as for us to understand the true factors leading to its success. We can, however, look to what we already know about remote work and apply these to a hybrid environment.

One of the ways that we can overcome the particular challenges of remote and hybrid work is to recognize how it is different to traditional office work, with which many of us are more familiar.

Trying to simply replicate our office lives in our homes, adopting the same ways of working, approaches and skills, may not lead to the best possible outcomes either for the individual, the team or the organization as a whole. For true effectiveness remote and hybrid workers need to take practical steps to create success, but also to rethink some of the very basics about how and when to work. Some of these new approaches can be undertaken on an individual basis, others will be best undertaken as a team. Identifying and working towards the necessary skills is the one key to creating success.

There is one final challenge relating to remote and hybrid work that is worth considering, and that is when the organization itself (including its managers) has its own culture or attitudes that may be a barrier to remote work. Not every organization that introduces remote work is entirely ready to do so. Not every manager that is required to lead a hybrid or remote team will truly believe in remote work, secretly preferring their team to be office-based. Although primarily organizational issues, remote workers need to be aware of the potential for these difficulties – and know how to navigate them. Some of these issues are tied up with myths about remote work.

Myths of remote work

There are plenty of myths relating to remote and hybrid work; some of them are false and some of them have some elements of truth – largely where success strategies are not employed.

Remote work isn't as effective as working in person

The belief that work has to take place in person, or will be much better in person, is a pervading one. However, the Covid-19 pandemic-enforced home working period showed us that it is perfectly possible for entire businesses to be run from home and still innovate, deliver and grow. Working virtually is different – but it does not have to be lesser.

Remote workers are hard to manage

Managing a remote team is different from managing a co-located team – but it does not necessarily mean that it is more difficult. It does, however, require adaption of approach and some new management and leadership skills. This subject will be explored more, later.

Physical distance also leads to psychological distance

Just because people are dispersed, undertaking their work in different places, some people assume that this will lead to a poorer experience, especially when it comes to working relationships and engagement with company culture. This *could* be true – when appropriate strategies are not in use – but is far from a guaranteed negative outcome.

Remote meetings aren't as good as in-person meetings

This is a variation on the first myth. Once again, there is little evidence to support this belief. Remote meetings, however, do need to be managed well – and differently – from an in-person meeting. This will also be explored later in this book. Remote meetings also have certain advantages over in-person meetings; they can be recorded for those who can't be present, they can be more accessible to people who can't join in person and they can even be live-streamed for greater participation.

People need to work together in person to innovate or collaborate

As we have already discussed, there is plenty of evidence from the pandemic that organizations continued to innovate and individuals collaborated effectively in a remote way. There are also many organizations that are entirely remote, and operate effectively and creatively.

People who work remotely aren't as committed to their careers

This is an unfortunate belief that is often attributed to people who work flexibly, including remote work, and it is usually referred to as flexible working stigma. There is no evidence to suggest that this is the case.

Remote workers will take advantage of being less visible

Another myth that lacks evidence, this was a common reason for turning down requests for remote (and other forms of flexible) work in the past. During the global pandemic this myth was very much exposed as there was no suggestion that businesses everywhere were facing an epidemic of laziness or skiving.

Remote work is isolating

Remote work can be isolating – but it doesn't have to be. It does, however, require both remote workers and their leaders to be intentional about making meaningful connections and building relationships.

It's hard to balance work and life when working remotely

It is true that it *can* be hard to find a work–life balance when working from home in particular – but this does not have to be the case when appropriate strategies are applied.

Remote work has a negative impact on careers

Unfortunately, this is another myth that does have an element of truth – largely because of some of the negative perceptions of remote workers by those who believe that in-person work is preferable. As we will explore later, remote workers need to put intentional focus on developing and progressing their own careers while working remotely.

Reflect

Do you believe any of these myths? If so, where do you think these beliefs come from, and what evidence do you have to support them? How might these beliefs impact upon your ability to be a successful remote worker? Which myth, if believed by others, could derail your success?

Where there are some potential elements of truth among these myths, presenting a possible risk to remote and hybrid workers, this book will explore how to address and mitigate them.

Skills for remote work

Many of the skills required to create success when working remotely or from home will already be familiar to you; they are often those same skills that support professional success in almost any working environment and are found in many job descriptions. However, the nature of remote work does mean that some of those skills take on greater importance than in a traditional office environment, or they need to be applied in new or different ways. Whether working from home some or all of the time, here are just some of the skills critical for home and remote working success:

- **Time management.** Remote workers must learn to manage their own time effectively without the structures and routines of an office environment and without guidance from a co-located manager or team.

- **Communication.** Remote work relies on effective communication, so remote workers must have the written and verbal communication skills to support success in a virtual environment. Good communication isn't enough for remote workers – excellent communication is the standard.

- **Collaboration.** This is all about people working together to achieve a common goal or purpose, or simply on a shared piece of work. Effective collaboration as a skill does not stand alone; it requires the application of many of the other skills listed here. Great collaborators are also good listeners, respectful of the opinions and contributions of others, and are open to ideas and challenge. Remote work does not mean working alone – it means working with others in a different way.

- **Relationship building.** Remote workers need to be able to build strong, trusting working relationships without necessarily being able to meet colleagues in person. Effective relationships contribute to many of the other skills listed here, including communication and collaboration.

- **Personal effectiveness.** Remote work is typically unsupervised work, on a day-to-day basis at least, so workers need to be self-motivated, highly organized, able to work independently and manage their time well.

- **Work–life balance management.** Without the boundaries of a typical office working day, remote workers need to employ a range of strategies to ensure that they can maintain a healthy work–life balance, avoiding falling foul of some of the well-being challenges that can arise.

- **Proactivity.** Remote workers need to be able to take the initiative and find solutions to their own challenges. There may not be a colleague at the next desk, or even in the same time zone, of whom questions can be asked, so workers will need to be proactive and resourceful.

- **Digital literacy.** Most remote work can only be undertaken by using technology. Workers need to be skilful users of a range of tools and systems. This is one more skill where 'good' simply isn't enough; tech skills need to be extensive, up to date and well applied.

- **Emotional intelligence.** Generally described as the ability to manage one's own emotions, to understand how behaviour influences others, and to perceive emotions in others. High levels of emotional intelligence can support relationship building; it can also help remote workers in particular to pick up emotional cues at a distance.

It is important to recognize that remote and home working isn't for everyone. This may be because the individual does not have the skills set out above. They may not feel that they are able to overcome the challenges of remote work. Some people find that it is too isolating, or that there is too little separation between work and home. Others will simply not have the space to create an acceptable working environment, or their home or family situation is not suitable. Before starting to work from home you may want to think carefully about whether it will work for you and your particular circumstances.

Many organizations provide support and training for remote workers, including help with establishing work–life balance or using relevant technology – this can help those who do not yet have the necessary skill set to develop it. Sometimes a trial period may be needed to establish suitability. With a hybrid working pattern it can all be about experimenting to find the right remote/office balance.

Skills for hybrid work

In many respects the skills for hybrid work are the same as for remote work. There are, however, some differences worthy of consideration. First of all, hybrid workers get the benefits of time working remotely and time working in the office. This makes it potentially easier to overcome some of the challenges of remote work, like managing visibility and building new colleague relationships. Hybrid workers do need to think differently about how they structure their working time and working week so that they are most effective at the right time and in the right place. They also need to be highly organized, particularly with regard to diary management. Hybrid workers will need to consider what work is best done where, what meetings should be held face to face versus virtually and how to manage a mix of remote and in-person relationships. This is likely to vary significantly from role to role, and organization to organization.

Hybrid workers need to be equally skilled in two sometimes contrasting skills; they need to be effective independent workers for their remote working time *and* strong team players during their collaborative working days. They need to be agile, and capable of switching between different ways of working according to the day, task or activity.

Hybrid workers will need to be skilled communicators – as much if not more so than entirely remote workers – comfortable with swapping from one form of communication to another seamlessly depending on where they are working. When meetings are hybrid (with mixed remote and in-person attendance) they will also need to be skilled facilitators and contributors. Leaders of hybrid teams must be alert to the complexities of hybrid; the conflict or lack of cohesion that may emerge between different groups working in different ways, and ensuring inclusion of all – wherever they work. Hybrid team managers will also need to learn how to manage their own unconscious biases and challenge their personal beliefs about remote and hybrid work, while ensuring they do not favour those who spend more time in the office over those who spend more time at work. Just like their fully remote counterparts, hybrid workers need to be proactive, good at managing their own work–life balance and have a high degree of digital literacy.

Above all, hybrid workers need to find balance – not just in their work and life but between their office and remote days, tasks and activities.

Whatever form of remote work is undertaken, there are some factors that are in the control or influence of the individual. This includes their skill set, behaviour, how they communicate and collaborate, productivity and even personal motivation. While there are some factors that are not in their control, such as the technologies provided by their organization, their manager or company systems and procedures, the good news for remote and hybrid workers is that there is much that is within their personal gift – from how they get ready to work remotely to their personal productivity.

Reflect

How ready are you to work remotely or in a hybrid way? Do you have the necessary skills to do so? If you are not sure how ready you are, refer to the 'Remote Work Readiness Assessment' in Appendix 1 (1) where you will find some questions upon which to reflect.

If you are reading this book because you would like to work from home but do not currently have the opportunity to do so, you will also find some tips on making an application to work remotely in Appendix 1 (2) 'Making a Remote Working Request'.

Summary points

- Remote work increased as a result of the global Covid-19 pandemic. This helped organizations to realize the potential of remote work and there was a strong demand from employees for continued remote work opportunities. Hybrid is a new form of remote working arising from the pandemic, where employees spend some time working in the office and some time from home.

- The broad nature of remote and hybrid work, varying from completely remote with no face-to-face working at all through to just an occasional day working from home, means that there is no simple best practice to adopt for remote working success in every situation. We should not treat remote work as one specific activity. Different strategies and approaches will be needed for different levels of remote working.

- Remote working can bring both benefits and challenges. Workers will need strategies to make the most of the opportunities of remote work while overcoming the potential difficulties.

- Remote work does not require a whole new skill set – many of the skills that will create remote work success are already those that support professional success. Those skills may, however, need to be employed in a different way.

- Remote and hybrid work success involve both technical skills and behavioural traits. Hybrid work requires very similar skills to remote work – but there are also some important differences to take into account. Remote work isn't for everyone – some will prefer (or be more successful in) the structure of a more traditional environment.

02
The practicalities of remote work

Setting yourself up for success

Ode of the first things that any remote or home worker needs to do is set themselves up to work effectively from home. Practical step number one is to establish an effective home working environment. However, before we get to this point, there is a critical question to consider: How remote are you?

> **Reflect**
>
> How remote are you? Remote work is not one single activity. The concept covers varying levels of remoteness from 100 per cent to occasional. The greater the level of remote activity, the more important some of the advice in this book becomes, demanding a higher focus and level of intentionality on getting remote right. Similarly, the greater the level of remoteness, the greater the potential for some of the challenges of remote work, identified in the previous chapter, to materialize.

Remote workstations

When people work from home only on an occasional basis it can be tempting to think that a dedicated working space isn't required and that they can work from temporary spaces like the dining table. This might be suitable if home working only takes place every so often, but long term this is not a good solution for a number of reasons. Poor ergonomics, such as not having an appropriate chair or desk, can lead to musculoskeletal issues like back pain or neck strain. Remote work can be even more sedentary than working in an office, with long hours of sitting unbroken by a commute or even a walk to a meeting room.

Working in a 'home' space such as a kitchen or lounge can also result in blurred boundaries between work and home which can be a source of conflict or stress; we will explore this subject more in a later chapter. Wherever possible, remote workers should create a separate space for their work activities, and always invest in a quality chair and desk. A good chair is one that is fully adjustable, has an arm rest and will support back and shoulder alignment. When seated to work, feet should be flat on the floor, and screens at eye level with work tools like keyboard and mouse in easy reach. Ideally a workspace should have natural daylight without any screen glare. These are simple tips but too often forgotten – both at home and in the office. It is also worth considering that a home workspace can be very different to the bland offices many of us are used to – remote workers can take the opportunity to use colour, light, plants or pictures to create a comfortable and engaging space.

Also give consideration to managing noise, positioning the workspace for natural daylight (a mood enhancer) and creating a clutter-free environment. Studies have shown that having too much clutter around the home or a workspace can raise levels of the stress hormone cortisol – meaning that a tidy desk and occasional declutter can be good remote strategies.

Do not underestimate the importance of creating a good (and comfortable) home working environment – it can be a key contributor to effectiveness, and therefore remote working success.

Working from home can result in large amounts of sitting throughout the working day. Regular breaks to stretch the body and rest eyes from screens are also important to reduce fatigue and eye strain.

Personal remote workspaces should also ensure privacy and data security – including adherence to any company-specific rules and requirements. No one else should ever have access to a remote worker's equipment or information. Always check any relevant company policies on these subjects.

Once a suitable workstation is set up the next step is to ensure a strong wifi connection – this is a prerequisite of working from home. A poor connection can seriously limit an individual's ability to work effectively as well as present a professional image. Unfortunately, it is also sometimes outside of an individual's control as wifi strength can be influenced by a range of factors. Where possible an investment may be required, either for superfast broadband where available, or booster devices.

Many organizations will have policies and procedures relating to home and remote working. These will typically include responsibilities and requirements; remote workers should be sure to familiarize themselves with these and seek further advice if they need further clarity on any points. In addition to formal policies, it is also common to find that teams or departments have their own local arrangements and rules relating to remote working. These may have been formally documented or are just generally understood; it is equally important for remote workers to become familiar with both.

Technology and digital tools

Home working technology will vary from organization to organization. It will typically include technology for online meetings such as Zoom and Microsoft Teams (which also has additional collaboration functionality), internal social media platforms like Yammer or Workplace, places for informal conversations like Slack or Teams, or places for collaboration on documents such as SharePoint.

Over time, specific technologies will change and evolve. The particular technology in use at any time or at any organization therefore is less relevant for home working success than building all-round technical competencies and a positive attitude towards keeping technology skills up to date. The increase in remote and home working following the pandemic led to the rapid development of new tech solutions. Many organizations will also use multiple different technology solutions to support remote or hybrid work.

Technology and communication, explored more in Chapter 4, go hand in hand. When working remotely, technology is the primary method for communicating and collaborating. Its use therefore needs to be planned and organized for it to be used to best effect. A variety of tools for remote collaboration are discussed later in this chapter; having good remote technology skills is about more than simply being competent with the best-known remote meeting platforms.

In terms of technology and digital tools, remote workers need to:

- Be aware of new technologies coming on stream and take proactive steps to learn how to use them.

- Be able to choose the best technology for the particular remote task – this is discussed in more detail later in this book.

- Know when to use technology to complete a particular task, or when a non- or low-tech approach is better, such as a phone call or conversation around a whiteboard.

- Where appropriate, help others they work with to use remote working technology – this helps a team to be more effective overall, which is also good for the individual worker.

- Manage their digital well-being when using a wide range of work-based technologies – this will be discussed more in Chapter 5 on well-being.

Reflect

What technologies are in use in your organization to enable remote and home working? How competent are you in using these technologies? What development needs do you have, and how can these be addressed?

After the set-up

Once the workstation is set up and the basics of remote work are in place, the next step in your remote work success is to consider how to make remote and hybrid work optimal, including how to adapt from the traditional office-based structure with which we are all familiar. The framework below provides some further context.

Baker (2021) describes four dimensions of work:

1 working together, together (such as collaborating in a meeting room on a shared task)

2 working together, apart (working at the same time but virtually through technology, such as an online meeting)

3 working alone, together (working in the same place, but undertaking independent work, such as sitting in an open plan office sending emails)

4 working alone, apart (working remotely and undertaking independent work, such as working from home and focusing on deep work)

We are very used to the first and third dimensions as these reflect the office as a default working place. This is the environment in which many current professionals learnt how to be successful at work. We know how to navigate these dimensions; how to build relationships there, manage our activities, communicate with others and manage our own careers. Many of us are perhaps less familiar with dimension 2, although we became much more so during the global pandemic. It might be easy to assume that during the pandemic we became suitably skilled to work remotely. We should not, however, fail to recognize the very real differences between working remotely during a crisis situation and remote work in its more normal form.

As we have already seen, there is no reason to assume that dimensions 1 and 3 should be the default for many of us, or that the other ways of working are not equally as effective.

Hybrid work is likely to involve at least three if not all four of these dimensions at different times. Success will therefore include the ability to be effective in each of them, *and* the ability to switch between them, determining which work should be done where. Fully remote work is likely to involve predominantly the second and fourth dimensions. The key to remote and hybrid work success is making each of these different dimensions of work as effective as possible, applying the remote work skills identified in Chapter 1.

Reflect

With which dimensions of work are you already familiar? In which dimensions have you already achieved career success? With which dimensions of work are you less familiar – and therefore where you need to focus more of your development?

This book will consider how to be successful in these new dimensions, taking each of the necessary skills and competencies in turn.

Building virtual relationships

Almost all work relies on relationships with others to some extent. These relationships might be with colleagues, peers, subordinates, customers or stakeholders. One of the most important relationships at work is of course the relationship between an employee and their immediate manager. Managers have the power to reward and recognize, provide opportunities and support career progression – it is therefore a key relationship to build in any environment, remote or co-located.

It is a myth that it is difficult to build relationships virtually. It does, however, require an adjusted approach plus more intentionality. Remote workers need to ensure that they don't

EXERCISE

Are you an effective remote collaborator?

Try asking yourself these questions:

- Do you offer your ideas or opinions in virtual meetings?
- Are you a confident facilitator when hosting virtual meetings?
- Do you feel confident to speak up in virtual meetings?
- Are you a competent user of a variety of remote collaboration technology tools?
- Are you confident you can be your authentic self when collaborating remotely?
- Do you listen effectively when collaborating remotely, managing distractions and avoiding multitasking?
- Do you contribute thoughtfully to discussions and activities in shared online spaces?
- Do you actively help to build trust and effective relationships in your team?
- Do you ask questions to build your own knowledge?
- Do you respond well to challenges or differences of opinions?

TOP TIPS

Set yourself up for success

- Talk to any other people you share a home with, if this will be your main remote base. This might include setting some expectations or ground rules so that everyone is clear, helping to avoid miscommunication or conflict. This is especially important if you have not worked from home before.

- Make sure to have childcare or other caring responsibilities arranged in advance of remote work. It isn't possible to do both at the same time and many organizations expressly prohibit it.

- Get to know your boss. Talk about expectations, working styles and the best way to communicate with each other.

- Check if your organization offers training on the various systems and technologies that are in use for remote work. Take steps to ensure you are fully able to utilize remote working technology.

- Make sure you understand your organization's policies or procedures relating to remote work. Check in with your manager about any local ways of working, documented or not.

- Check if your organization provides furniture for working from home, or an allowance to purchase your own. Even if they do not this is still an investment in your well-being that is worth making.

- If you are a new starter and one is not provided automatically, ask for a mentor or buddy to support you in your first weeks or months. Many organizations have mentoring schemes so check with any internal learning and development function. This will provide you with a colleague to whom you can pose quick questions.

- As a new starter, introduce yourself and let people know that you have recently joined the organization and would welcome the opportunity to meet with them and learn more about the work that they do.

- Reflect on when you are personally most productive – this might not be the traditional patterns worked in an office, which is usually 9 to 5 with an hour for lunch. There is more guidance on how to do this in Appendix 1 (5) on 'Identifying your Personal Productivity'.

forget informal conversations. Virtual meetings can lack the more social aspects of in-person meetings, such as chatting while people are arriving or during a coffee break. These interactions help people get to know one another, supporting the building of relationships. Make time for this; open meetings a few minutes early, start with a check-in or by asking people how they are or create some space in a meeting where there isn't an agenda item. One approach is to schedule relationship time. Every week dedicate some time for building and maintaining relationships; treat this with equal importance to completing work-based activities and tasks. Put the time in to get to know people and let them get to know you. Share a little about yourself – as much as you feel comfortable. Trust is also important for building professional relationships; this will be explored in more depth in Chapter 6.

Tip

The next time you have an online meeting with a colleague, intentionally focus on the relationship before the task. Ask them how they are, enquire about their weekend or their family, and make some space for non-work dialogue. It's tempting to get straight down to business, but this small time investment can deliver real relationship benefits.

Tip

Why not be the person that organizes a social event or activity for your team? Try Coffee Roulette – randomly matching colleagues for a weekly coffee break. This can help to connect people who don't usually meet each other, creating new relationships. Organizing activities like these can help to position you as a strong collaborator and build your visibility.

Relationships and hybrid work

Hybrid work provides the opportunity to build relationships both in person and virtually. Research suggests that when employees work remotely more than 2.5 days per week, there can be a moderate negative effect on co-worker relationships (Gajendran and Harrison, 2007). For the entirely remote or predominantly remote worker, this is more evidence for the need to place significant focus on building relationships. For the hybrid worker, this gives rise to another question, related to both working relationships but also other key areas of work: what is the most effective split of home versus office?

Unfortunately, there is no simple answer as this will vary from job to job and organization to organization. The research mentioned above suggests that from a relationship perspective a rough 50/50 split is ideal. Context, however, is key.

Collaborating remotely

In the discussion about skills for remote work in Chapter 1, collaboration was identified as a key skill for success. Collaboration is all about people working together to achieve a common goal or purpose, or simply on a particular piece of work – and in an entirely remote environment this has to be done virtually and through the use of technology. In the past it would have been very difficult to collaborate effectively when people were not co-located. Now there are many tools that can support effective collaboration – but the tools aren't enough on their own. Remote workers need to be expert collaborators. What does this mean in practice? Expert collaborators:

- listen attentively
- ask lots of questions and seek to understand
- are open to new ideas and challenges
- share willingly and generously

- are team-minded rather than focused on themselves

- communicate well and often

- want to work with others

None of these competencies or behaviours change as a result of working remotely – only the practicalities and the 'how' are different. Hybrid workers will have the opportunity to make a deliberate choice to collaborate in person, using their office-based time in which to do so. For the fully remote worker, collaboration will be virtual, using some of the technologies already discussed.

Tip

Many of the good practice advice for virtual collaboration is the same as for hosting or participating in virtual meetings. Review the guidance in Chapter 4 for more information and help.

To support effective remote collaboration, you should consider some of the following:

- Build trust in the team first – this will create what is known as psychological safety, where people feel it is okay to be themselves and share their opinions and feelings.

- Create a virtual collaboration space and process that is accessible to everyone. Think about timing, technology and working styles.

- Use the technology that fits the type of collaboration necessary (see the following section on 'Remote collaboration tools').

- Identify the best way to capture any output from collaboration activities.

- Find ways to include everyone in discussions and activities to ensure the widest possible voice and encourage diversity of thought.

Remember: not only does collaboration *not* have to take place in person for it to be effective, it also does not have to take place *at the same time*. We will explore this concept more in Chapter 5. Don't fall into the trap of believing collaboration can only take place in person, at the same time. This is just one way that work can get done.

If reflecting on any of these questions identifies a learning need, consider how you can build additional skills to ensure you are a successful remote collaborator.

Remote collaboration tools

The following tools and technologies can support virtual collaboration – new tools, however, are constantly being developed. Some of these are free technologies whereas others require a contract or subscription. Many have some free elements but full functionality is only available at cost:

- for meetings: MS Teams, Zoom, Google Meet, GoToMeeting
- for messaging: Slack, Chanty, MS Teams, WhatsApp
- for capturing ideas: Mural, Miro, Padlet, Invision Freehand, Jamboard
- for file sharing: Dropbox, MS Teams, Slack, Google Drive
- for project and task management: Trello, Slack, MS Teams, Chanty, Basecamp

Which tool will work best will depend on the team and the type of work being undertaken. Whichever tools are chosen, they should be used sensibly. No one wants to use more tools than are necessary for the task in hand – this adds complexity and can lead to notification overload.

EXERCISE

Are you an effective remote collaborator?

Try asking yourself these questions:

- Do you offer your ideas or opinions in virtual meetings?
- Are you a confident facilitator when hosting virtual meetings?
- Do you feel confident to speak up in virtual meetings?
- Are you a competent user of a variety of remote collaboration technology tools?
- Are you confident you can be your authentic self when collaborating remotely?
- Do you listen effectively when collaborating remotely, managing distractions and avoiding multitasking?
- Do you contribute thoughtfully to discussions and activities in shared online spaces?
- Do you actively help to build trust and effective relationships in your team?
- Do you ask questions to build your own knowledge?
- Do you respond well to challenges or differences of opinions?

TOP TIPS

Set yourself up for success

- Talk to any other people you share a home with, if this will be your main remote base. This might include setting some expectations or ground rules so that everyone is clear, helping to avoid miscommunication or conflict. This is especially important if you have not worked from home before.

- Make sure to have childcare or other caring responsibilities arranged in advance of remote work. It isn't possible to do both at the same time and many organizations expressly prohibit it.

- Get to know your boss. Talk about expectations, working styles and the best way to communicate with each other.

- Check if your organization offers training on the various systems and technologies that are in use for remote work. Take steps to ensure you are fully able to utilize remote working technology.

- Make sure you understand your organization's policies or procedures relating to remote work. Check in with your manager about any local ways of working, documented or not.

- Check if your organization provides furniture for working from home, or an allowance to purchase your own. Even if they do not this is still an investment in your well-being that is worth making.

- If you are a new starter and one is not provided automatically, ask for a mentor or buddy to support you in your first weeks or months. Many organizations have mentoring schemes so check with any internal learning and development function. This will provide you with a colleague to whom you can pose quick questions.

- As a new starter, introduce yourself and let people know that you have recently joined the organization and would welcome the opportunity to meet with them and learn more about the work that they do.

- Reflect on when you are personally most productive – this might not be the traditional patterns worked in an office, which is usually 9 to 5 with an hour for lunch. There is more guidance on how to do this in Appendix 1 (5) on 'Identifying your Personal Productivity'.

- Identify challenges you personally experience with time management and organization. Experiment with different approaches and techniques to find the one that works best for you. More information to support you with these can be found in Chapter 3.

- Consider using a tool to support prioritization and organization. As well as analogue approaches such as a notebook and a to-do list, there are a range of apps to support time management.

- Focus on enhancing your collaboration skills to ensure these are as effective as they can be.

Appendix 1 (3) provides more details of the main pitfalls to avoid when working remotely.

Summary points

- Remote workers should not underestimate the importance of setting up a comfortable and engaging home working space. This is good for well-being and productivity. Setting up for success also includes building relationships, effective collaboration and using technology.

- Technology is key – remote and hybrid workers need to ensure that they are fully competent with any technologies that are in use in their particular organization. These will inevitably change over time as new technologies are developed, so skills need to be kept up to date.

- There is no single way to set up remote or hybrid working success – even experienced remote workers may have to adapt their approach depending on organizational culture and the particular context within which they work.

03
Your personal productivity and effectiveness

Some managers fear that if their employees work from home this will lead to reduced productivity, and that employees would, without the supervision that is associated with in-person and office work, take advantage of the opportunity to do less work or malinger. However, many office environments are also full of distractions and are not necessarily suitable for people who are neurodiverse. In contrast, remote work can aid focus and concentration and can be especially helpful for those who need to undertake deep work.

Productivity is a personal concept; what makes one person productive will not necessarily hold true for another. Productivity, in many respects, is a feeling. Someone might feel that they have been productive if they have emptied their email inbox or finished a list of tasks on their to-do list. Someone else might feel productive if they have had one single, fantastic idea.

Reflect

What does productivity mean to you, in your role? Can you define it? How do you know if you have had a productive day? How does your organization or line manager define productivity? Defining productivity for ourselves and our particular role is a helpful starting point in ensuring that we are maximizing it. Appendix 1 (5) provides guidance on identifying your personal productivity.

There is no one single way of measuring productivity, although some jobs will lend themselves more easily to measurement through readily observable key performance indicators. Working from home demands organization and self-motivation. Individuals are responsible for their own performance and their own time, with no manager to account to, at least in the short term. For some this will come naturally whereas other remote workers will need to place considerable effort and time in getting this right. Appendix 1 (5) (Identifying your Personal Productivity) contains some questions to help remote workers to reflect on their own productivity and where and when they are most effective.

Rethinking time

Remote work allows us to do something radical; it allows us to rethink time. One of the very earliest definitions of remote work by academic Mancur Olson described it as 'work that is performed outside the normal organizational confines of space and time' (Olson, 1983). Even then, when technology was in its infancy and wifi in the distant future, remote work was seen as being about more than just location, but also about time.

Work is typically structured around time. Start times, end times, break times and lunch times. Our working time is often defined in formal documents like contracts of employment, issued to us by our employers. Some organizations will have rotas, shifts or flexi-time systems. Many also measure work times by requiring employees to clock on or off, or measuring the time they take to do tasks. The focus on time has a long tradition in management theory; at the heart of it is the very idea that work and time are interlinked. This does not, however, have to be the case – but the default working day, and the beliefs that have built up around it, are pervasive. Understanding these beliefs, and how to work with them and challenge them appropriately, can help to support remote work success.

The standard eight-hour working day is a throwback to the Industrial Revolution when work generally needed to be completed at a specific time and at a specific place. Time, task and place were bound together. The technologies that we take for granted in our daily lives today did not exist then; the advent of digital technology has enabled us to separate work from time and place, only not everyone has done so. Back in 1998, an article by Davenport and Pearlson in the *MIT Sloan Management Review* suggested that work was becoming 'something you do, not a place where you go'. Only in 2020 did we begin to realize this prediction.

The typical working week is generally structured around five days of eight hours – often 9 to 5 or a very close approximation. Usually there will be one break of around an hour in the middle of the day. This type of work (before remote work was a possibility) was formally separated from other parts of life by a commute at either end of that working day. Anyone who worked outside of that norm was somehow 'other', and sometimes stigmatized or looked down upon.

We will shortly have a discussion about more traditional forms of time management, but first let us consider how remote work allows us to really rethink working time.

We tend to conflate presence with performance, and time with productivity. Neither is necessarily true. We can be in the office or visible at a laptop without making a meaningful contribution. We can also put in long hours sitting at a desk, but achieve little in real terms.

Changing our mindset on time requires us to let go of some of our old beliefs about what is a good worker and where work is done. This will truly allow us to embrace the potential of remote work. This is not a simple ask. Not all organizations, or all managers, will be ready to think about time in this way and many remote workers will have to work within the confines of their organizational rules and requirements. Where autonomy is provided, however, the remote worker can seize this opportunity to truly create a work schedule that is personal and optimal for them and their unique circumstances.

Remember:

Time ≠ productivity

Presence ≠ performance

In their book on remote work, Chris Dyer and Kim Shepherd (2021) suggest thinking about the time gained through working remotely as a gift to self, something that can be used to enrich our lives or support our personal well-being. If we are to do so, however, we will have to challenge some of our own beliefs and tendencies, especially about how we should behave and how hard we should work. Remember Parkinson's Law: 'Work expands so as to fill the time available for its completion.' As we will explore in Chapter 5 on well-being, remote work in particular expands – into our home lives, if we are not organized in relation to our time.

Later in this chapter we will explore in more detail ideas about organizing our time. When reading these suggestions and materials, the remote worker should keep in mind the opportunities to personalize working patterns – the greater personalization we can achieve, the more likely we are to be satisfied with our work, have good well-being and be personally productive.

As well as rethinking time, remote and hybrid work challenges us to think more fundamentally too: just what is good work? Good work has often been aligned with working long hours. Instead, we should consider good work to be about personal performance, contribution, value created and outcomes generated. This too, is a mindset shift.

Reflect

Where do you have your best ideas? Is it your desk or your office, or somewhere else entirely? And if you have those ideas somewhere other than your desk, are you still working? Some people will have their best ideas while exercising, resting or even in the shower. Great work does not have to take place at an office – or even a desk.

Time management

Time management is simply about the way that we organize our activities and make sure that we are allocating the right amount of time to the right tasks. It is about being deliberate with our use of time and taking control over it. Time management sounds simple, but it isn't a skill that everyone has mastered. It is, as we have already identified, a key skill for remote work. When there is no one else managing someone's time (generally a manager) nor as much time structure to the working day (such as a train or bus to catch or a set lunchbreak), the remote worker has to manage time for themselves. The home worker also has to manage the distractions that might exist in the home, from a delivery interrupting flow to noise from other family members who are occupying the home at the same time.

Different people will struggle with different aspects of time management. For some, it is about having too many distractions in the remote environment or just simply too much work to do (or saying yes to too many things). Others find it difficult to plan ahead or prioritize work.

Reflect

How effective is your time management? Do you have any particular time management challenges when working remotely? What are your personal time management challenges that need to be overcome? How can you do this?

Procrastination is a familiar time management problem: the tendency to put off something important that needs to be done, often leaving it to the last minute, even when the procrastinator knows that this is only going to cause them future difficulties. It can also include putting off something important for something much less important, but that in the moment feels more interesting or exciting, such as putting off writing an important report in order to scroll social media.

Procrastination can occur for several different reasons. Some people are perfectionists, not finding it difficult to begin a task but to finalize it, possibly becoming too absorbed in detail. Other procrastinators are avoiding a task, possibly because they are worried about it, concerned about their competence or the potential for making mistakes. Some procrastinators simply thrive on the crisis or emergency that can result. Procrastination may be a general issue for an individual, or result only in relation to specific tasks or activities.

Reflect

What do you procrastinate over? Which tasks get left on your to-do list or unfinished – and why? In what circumstances are you more likely to procrastinate? Understanding our personal tendencies relating to procrastination can be the key to addressing it.

From a simple to-do list to online tools, there is a wide variety of time management tools available; no single tool will work for every individual. Remote workers who want to manage their time well will need to do two things:

- understand their own specific time management challenges
- experiment with different ways of managing time when working remotely, to identify the best possible personal approach

Effective time management is about working smarter, not harder – or longer hours.

Time management techniques

Try some of these simple techniques that can support your remote working effectiveness. These techniques can also work well in an office-based environment. However, some, like the Pomodoro technique (see the box), can be especially helpful in supporting focus and time management when working independently.

First of all, remote workers need to plan their day in advance. This is even more crucial for the hybrid worker, who may find that their remote working day is very different to their office-based working day. Effective time management includes:

- **Prioritization.** Addressing the most important and urgent tasks first, and not necessarily those that other people think are urgent and important, or those that have been outstanding the longest. A standard to-do list can help with this but only if the tasks are ranked in order of importance.
- **Tracking time.** Identifying where time is being spent, or indeed where it is being wasted or not used to best effect, is key to effective remote time management.
- **Delegation.** Remote workers need to know what they should be working on and what needs to be passed on to colleagues or team members.

- **Managing distractions**. Always part of time management, the home office can be full of distractions which need to be overcome for effectiveness. However, the office is full of distractions too – albeit the distractions are often different in nature.

EXERCISE
The Pomodoro technique

Developed by Francesco Cirillo, this technique is named after a tomato-shaped kitchen timer!

When preparing to undertake a particular task, prevent any disruptions such as email or message notifications. Set a timer and focus entirely on the task at hand for 20 minutes. When the timer goes off, take a 10-minute break. Repeat at least three times (Pomodoro sets). Experiment with different times to determine the optimal personal pattern.

This exercise is designed to support focus – it can be much easier to implement when working remotely than in an office environment where interruptions are harder to prevent.

Some remote workers may find it helpful to use a time management or productivity tool or app. There are a wide range on the market and it is likely that some will work better than others for specific individuals and their working styles. Examples you might wish to consider include:

- Focus Keeper: similar to the Pomodoro technique, this app has a timer function
- Toggle: to help identify where time is spent
- MindNode: which can help capture thoughts and ideas visually
- MyLifeOrganized: for managing tasks, to-do lists and goals
- Focus@Will: uses specifically designed music to support focus – especially helpful for those who may experience attention deficit disorders

- Evernote: a tool to keep files and notes in one place in the cloud, making them accessible from anywhere

- Pocket: for saving and organizing web-based content for easy reference

There are also apps and settings on mobile devices that allow notifications from apps to be temporarily silenced, or alerts when too much time has been spent on particular websites or platforms.

Remote and hybrid workers may also benefit from time blocking. This simply refers to intentional diary management, where blocks of time are scheduled into the diary to complete specific tasks. The block of time dedicated should be appropriate to the task and should be long enough to make meaningful progress without being over long.

Tip

Take control of your diary to ensure you get breaks and thinking time. Block out space in your diary where you will not accept any meetings. If you don't block out the time – someone will take it! If you do time block you may need to tell people (such as your boss) that you are doing this and why.

Later on in this book we will consider the importance of visibility for reputation and career development. However, this needs to be balanced with the need for focused time and planned work. Being visible is important – but needs to be balanced with scheduling and managing time effectively, and not being 'always on'.

Taking breaks

Planning work also includes planning breaks – as highlighted in the previous section, breaks should be ideally scheduled into the diary, and long enough to provide an appropriate rest. Breaks support focus and well-being, and provide a recovery period from work. We recover from work in two ways: in short breaks from work such as a few minutes away from our desk to stretch or take a walk, or in longer periods of downtime such as holidays and weekends. Everyone needs an element of both types of rest. Breaks also need to include an element of meaningful disconnecting from work technology. It's not a break to move away from the desk but continue to check messages on another device.

Working hours

When working remotely it can be helpful to set some established or regular working hours. In fact, some remote working advice suggests that replicating the office routine is a good thing, as it can help to provide valuable structure and establish boundaries between work and home. Not everyone, however, will benefit from this approach; productivity, well-being and working styles are personal and contextual.

However, having some structure around working hours creates a routine, and helps remote workers to know when to stop work and helps to manage work–life balance. There is no reason, however, why these hours need to be the traditional 9 to 5, or in the case of hybrid workers, the same hours worked on office-based days. Similarly, when working remotely there is no need necessarily to reflect the pattern of the office day of a one-hour break halfway through the day. Remote work allows for personalization. But we are often so conditioned to work an eight-hour day around 9 to 5 that it can be a difficult habit to break. We can be *time* flexible as well as *location* flexible.

Whenever someone chooses to work it is generally good practice not to work late into the night. When working from home it might be tempting to work in the evenings. However, this can stimulate our brain, especially if working with devices that emit blue light, negatively impacting upon our sleep and therefore our recovery from work. Poor sleep may mean that we are insufficiently rested to work effectively the following day.

> **Reflect**
>
> *When* are you most effective? What working hours most suit your working style and the type of work that you do? Do you need anyone to agree these hours?

Managing your hybrid schedule

When a team is co-located in an office environment and works there by default, there is not necessarily a requirement to think strategically about what type of work to do at any particular time. We may simply respond to what emails arrive, attend meetings in person or tackle our to-do list in order. When work is entirely remote this may also be the case.

There are additional added complexities in a hybrid-type environment, where individuals spend some time in an office and some time from home. We have to think purposefully about what work to do where – and when. When working in a hybrid way there can be a real benefit in structuring work differently, scheduling independent or highly focused work for home, and work that is more collaborative or relationship-focused for the office. More planning and focus is required than in the default office setting – we will discuss this in more depth later in this chapter.

When working remotely combined with an aspect of time flexibility there is also a need to think not just about where to work but when to work, as freedom from commuting and rigid office days allows for that greater personalization.

When working in a hybrid way, taking some time to plan the week ahead can help remote workers to optimize their time and effectiveness. Having a plan might seem like an unnecessary step for experienced professionals, but it can help to provide focus and clarity as well as enhance productivity.

Hybrid workers should carefully consider which are the best days to be in the office, and which are the best days to be remote, based on the nature of the work and their own personal working styles. Some employees will have autonomy over this whereas others may not. Should a hybrid schedule be fixed or variable?

Working the same pattern each week

- provides certainty and consistency for colleagues and stakeholders
- allows for the scheduling of regular meetings and events in person or virtually
- provides structure and can support boundaries and work–life balance
- enables employees to manage caring responsibilities more effectively
- might be easier for the individual's manager to coordinate
- can make personal work planning easier

However, such a schedule might also be unnecessarily rigid, involve attending the office when it isn't really essential and can also result in collaborating mainly with other people who are also undertaking the same fixed schedule rather than with the broader team.

Variable schedules

- allow employees to have greater flexibility to adapt to organizational needs, potentially benefitting both them and the organization
- will provide greater autonomy to the individual – which is good for engagement and motivation
- ensures that there is no wasted time commuting when there is no need to do so
- allows more personalization and autonomy for the individual
- can provide the opportunity for interaction with a wide group of colleagues (especially when everyone works a varied schedule)

With a variable schedule it might be tempting not to go into the office on a Friday – this has always been a popular work-from-home day. This might, however, not be the best day for the organization, colleagues or stakeholders. Hybrid workers should think carefully about their hybrid schedule – there is no 'best' approach, only the most appropriate one for the circumstance.

The following factors are relevant:

- the individual and their personal working preferences and style
- the role itself, and the required duties and responsibilities
- productivity and effectiveness
- other people – including team, manager, customers and stakeholders
- work–life balance and well-being
- suitability of working environments, either at home or in the office

Sometimes, these different aspects will align, but sometimes they will not and compromises will need to be made. Hybrid workers should consider:

- what organization or team policies exist about requirements to attend the office
- what schedule is most suitable, taking into account the different factors set out above
- where they are most productive and add the most value
- which tasks are most suited to which working environment
- when other colleagues are working
- what pattern will support career and professional success longer term, e.g. what days will support learning and development or access to opportunities
- what works for the worker's manager and establishing an effective relationship with them

- what *time* schedule will suit them, as well as location schedule

- what schedule will provide the most contact with colleagues or other key stakeholders

- whether the schedule needs to be agreed in advance with anyone else

Reflect

Where are you most effective for which tasks? If you work in a hybrid way, which of your tasks are best completed with others or in the office, and which are best undertaken independently when remote?

EXERCISE
Identifying effective hybrid working patterns

Hybrid work can take many forms. It may involve working half the time in the office and half remotely. It may also include a pattern that changes from week to week or month to month. Some hybrid work may be mostly at home with only a small period of time co-located with colleagues – or vice versa. Some employees will have more autonomy than others in determining their hybrid pattern. Establishing an optimal schedule may take some experimentation.

Consider some of the following questions to help you to identify appropriate and effective hybrid working patterns:

- What can you determine for yourself regarding your schedule, and what do you need to agree with your manager?

- When and where do you feel that you are most effective and productive?

- What aspects of your work can be undertaken most effectively at home?

- What aspects of your work can be undertaken most effectively in the office/co-located with others?
- Where do you or your work gain value from being in the office?
- What specific tasks are suited to independent work and what tasks require collaboration?
- How should you organize your work accordingly?

Managers of hybrid teams should give careful consideration to the need for fixed or variable schedules. Generally, the greater autonomy provided to employees, the better this will be for engagement, motivation and well-being. However, this will not always be possible depending on the type of work undertaken and the needs of the organization. Whatever decision is made about hybrid schedules, transparency is key. To ensure that employees feel that they have been treated fairly, share any relevant organizational policies with them and explain clearly why decisions about hybrid schedules have been made. Above all, employees should know exactly what is expected of them.

Improving focus

Mindfulness

Mindfulness can be a useful tool for boosting focus. Although not a new concept by any means, mindfulness has become increasingly popular in recent years. Essentially, mindfulness is about being fully present in the current moment. It is a practice designed to help individuals to become more aware of their feelings and emotions without judgement. There is a focus on the breath as a technique for staying in the present moment.

Research has found that mindfulness can support remote workers by helping them to disconnect from work, but crucially also to improve their attention to work tasks. It can help remote workers to manage competing demands for attention, stop the mind from wandering and sharpen focus. These aren't the only benefits from practising mindfulness. It has also been found helpful in reducing negative thoughts and pessimistic thinking and supports well-being and good mental health. Mindfulness is, however, not a magic bullet. It does need to be undertaken regularly for maximum benefits to be realized. For the remote worker who recognizes that they need help in achieving focus and not becoming distracted, undertaking a regular mindfulness practice can bring significant benefits.

There are a range of tools either freely or cheaply available online or via downloadable apps that can support individuals in learning simple mindfulness techniques. Simple mindful meditations, some lasting for just a few minutes, can help remote workers to bring their attention to their current thoughts and feelings and improve their focus.

Tip

Search online for mindfulness podcasts or guided meditations. Try a range of different examples and reflect on whether they help you to increase your focus and attention.

Motivation

Generally, remote work and motivation go hand in hand. Remote work by its very nature has a large degree of autonomy; there is less clock watching and supervision, and workers are often responsible for their own schedule. We know from Daniel Pink's seminal work *Drive* (2010) that people aren't necessarily motivated by money and rewards, but instead by autonomy, mastery (the ability or urge to improve or enhance skills) and purpose (doing something that has meaning). Autonomy is about being self-directed and independent, with freedom to choose, especially in relation to how work is done. Simply, most people don't like being micro-managed or told what to do.

However, although many people enjoy working remotely or from home, that doesn't necessarily mean they will always feel motivated or engaged. Remote work demands an element of self-motivation – particularly when the type of remote work is highly independent. Motivation is quite a personal concept; what motivates one person will not necessarily motivate another. There is therefore an element of self-awareness required from the remote worker. A few simple techniques can help:

- **Set daily and weekly goals or challenges.** As you complete them this can help generate a feeling of accomplishment.
- **Build in breaks.** This is good for well-being but will also support energy levels and avoid fatigue.
- **Build some learning into the work week.** This can help us to feel that we are progressing and developing.
- **Take some time to reflect** on what has gone well during the day or week. A little positive psychology or deliberate gratitude is a mood booster.
- **Eat frogs!** This is a common time management technique – the idea being that if you have to eat a frog, you might as well do it quickly and get it out of the way. Having unfinished work hanging over us can be a demotivator.
- **Do something enjoyable.** Working from home provides opportunities that the office does not. Go for a lunchtime walk or do an exercise class. Make a healthy lunch or engage in a hobby during the time you would have been commuting.
- **Reward yourself** when you complete a good piece of work. A short break, a cup of quality coffee or just something simple and enjoyable can also provide a motivation boost.

EXERCISE
Getting motivated

If you find that you regularly feel demotivated when working remotely, take some time out to think about why this might be, and what you can change to help you feel more motivated and purposeful. Try a few of these self-coaching questions:

- Who can I talk to for advice and support?
- What would make me feel more motivated right now?
- What small steps could I take today that would help me to feel more motivated?
- What habits can I create to support my motivation?

Experiment with different work routines and options to see what works for you.

Managing distractions

As we have already discussed, working from home will require remote workers to manage distractions. This will not be a new skill set for many who have worked in offices – arguably offices have more distractions than a remote environment, especially where that office is open plan. At home, the distractions are simply different. They might involve other family members, neighbours or the constant ping of electronic notifications.

There is no best practice way to manage distractions. What distracts one person will have no impact upon another. A tool for managing them may be found useful by some but not others. For example, some people find background music helpful whereas others will find it irritating. The extent to which we are distracted, or can manage those distractions, will also be influenced by the type of work that we are doing at any particular time and even our own personality type.

EXERCISE
Managing distractions

Remote and hybrid workers may wish to experiment with different ways to manage distractions to identify what works for them. The following questions can aid reflection:

- What distractions may arise in your remote working environment?
- What control do you have over these distractions?
- What can you try that will help you to overcome these particular distractions?
- What supports your concentration?
- What do you need to put in place to prevent you being disturbed while working remotely?
- What do you need to ask others to do, in order to support you with managing your distractions?

Review some of the other techniques discussed in this chapter in relation to focus and time management to help you with managing distractions while undertaking remote work.

Summary points

- Remote and hybrid work allows us to rethink time. It enables us to tailor work to personal preferences and style, which can in turn support well-being and work–life balance.
- Presence, time and productivity are not the same – but are often conflated.
- Productivity is personal. There is a great deal of advice about productivity, as well as many different tools and techniques to support being productive. Remote and hybrid workers will

need to reflect on their own personal productivity, preferences and working style in order to identify what works for them and their specific situation.

- Time management is a key skill for remote or hybrid workers as they are predominantly responsible for their own time without the structure provided by the office environment or daily commute.

- Remote and hybrid workers are also responsible for their own motivation and managing distractions. There are multiple techniques for each: the starting point for remote and hybrid workers is self-awareness and reflection.

- Hybrid workers have different challenges to remote workers: hybrid work involves working in different places at different times, demanding that the individual is able to plan and schedule their work to ensure they are effective wherever they are working.

04
Communication and collaboration

Communication is fundamentally about sharing information and generating shared understanding. It is a key skill for professional life, whether work takes place in person or virtually.

When working in the office, communication can be spontaneous and ad hoc. There is generally a mix of electronic and in-person communication. When working remotely, the majority of communication takes place via technology, whether that is email, messaging systems or a virtual meeting. Electronic communication includes so many different ways of communicating, from an email, a WhatsApp or text message to an update on a social media platform or even an emoji or a 'like'. This can lead to an increased volume of communication that all needs to be managed, with messages arriving through a variety of online channels. Each of these different forms have their own rules, levels of formality and nuances.

Remote communication is also fundamentally different to in-person communication; body language and non-verbal cues are reduced, as is informal and casual communication. These missing cues, plus the fact that a lot of communication when working remotely is written, mean that there is a greater potential for misunderstandings and a loss of important emotional context. Communicators within remote teams need to be mindful of this and adapt approaches accordingly to minimize this risk.

Remote workers therefore need exceptional communication skills, and they also need to be able to manage the sometimes high volume of different communications that are flowing to them as they work. In the remote world, we need to communicate with care – with both the message and the medium. Remote working success requires an individual to learn strategies for managing each of these issues.

Being an effective remote communicator includes:

- **Listening well.** Listening may sound like a skill that we all already have. Not everyone, however, is an *effective* listener. It is possible to be physically present at a conversation but not be actively listening (consider the online meeting in which participants are clearly multitasking!). Our daily lives provide many barriers to effective listening, with technology being a particular problem area.

- **Questioning skills.** Asking good questions elicits information, helps promote shared understanding, prompts thinking and reflection and can help us get to know other people and their perspectives. Each of these supports the communication process.

- **Feedback.** Effective communicators can provide meaningful feedback and do so in a timely and constructive way.

- **Body language.** A significant proportion of the way that we communicate is non-verbal and involves our body language, eye contact and tone of voice.

- **Selecting the appropriate communication medium** for a particular communication. Being able to determine when, where and how to use which method of communication is part of the skill of communicating itself.

- **Understanding the delicate balance** between over- and under-communicating.

- **Thinking about every stage in the process.** Strong communicators consider their role as the sender of the message as well as the needs of the recipient. Whether communicating in writing or verbally, formally or informally, care is taken throughout. Excellent communicators work to build shared understanding, reduce miscommunication and address barriers to communication. Good communication doesn't just happen – it is planned and managed.

EXERCISE
Developing your communication skills

How effective are your communication skills? Are there any specific challenges you experience when communicating remotely compared to in person? Do you have any areas for development and how can you address them? If you are not sure, consider some of the questions below:

- Are you able to use a variety of communication tools to undertake your communication?

- Are you aware of the communication preferences of the people you work with and your manager?

- Are you respectful of time differences if working in a globally distributed team?

- Do you consider the best way to communicate a message (such as email, instant messaging system or in a virtual meeting)?

- Before communication, do you consider the potential for misunderstandings or miscommunication?

- Are you an effective virtual presenter, or virtual meeting host?

- Are you aware of the potential challenges of communicating in a remote environment – and do you take positive steps to address these?

If you have answered 'no' to any of these questions, consider what you need to do in order to address this area.

The right communication approach for you

Part of being an effective communicator is determining the most appropriate way of communicating for any particular message or activity. There are many different factors to take into account. One key communication decision is deciding between synchronous and asynchronous communication (discussed below). Another related aspect is deciding between the type of media – whether to use lean media (a medium that is often quick but conveys less information and context, such as a text message) or rich media which has more depth and carries more information, such as a video. Face-to-face communication is generally the richest form of communication medium. We often think that this makes it the best but this is not necessarily the case. What really matters is matching the type of communication to the situation, audience and message itself. Messages might be simple or complex. Urgent or routine. Messages may generate emotion or be neutral. They may require inter-pretation and processing, requiring time for the recipient to reflect and consider, or they might be simple and straightforward. All of these factors should be taken into account when deciding how to communicate.

Asynchronous communication simply refers to communication that does not take place in real time. It is often a lean medium and can include emails, using message platforms, writing blogs, videos or collaborating on documents in a shared space at different times. Responses to questions or requests for information will not neces-sarily be immediate. In contrast, synchronous (real-time) commu-nication takes place when people are working together, such as meetings, and is often a rich medium.

The most appropriate medium for communicating any particular message also depends on what you need people to do with the information. Research into communication processes differentiates between two broad types of communication: conveying information and converging on meaning (Dennis et al, 2008). Conveying information refers to the transmission of information, and can often be achieved with lean media. It is about telling people things that they need to know. Converging on meaning is more complex. It involves discussion, processing and agreeing. It will involve interaction and back and forth conversation. It includes sense-making. Some communication messages will involve only conveying information, others will involve a mix of both processes. Information being conveyed only can therefore suit a lean medium, whereas the need to convey meaning demands a richer one.

The best communication medium therefore is the one that best fits the situation, and will inevitably involve a combination of considerations relating to the sender of the communication, the message and the recipient. Often more than one communication medium is required. For example, rich synchronous provision of information via an online meeting followed by an asynchronous space for comment and questions. No one channel or approach is likely to meet every need, and communication needs will also change over time.

The challenges of remote communication

Remote communication can bring with it specific challenges including:

- Recipients of communications (especially through meetings) might multitask during the receiving process, reducing their ability to listen to the message.

- Misunderstandings, especially through electronic communication where other cues are absent.

- Communication overload (too many messages and notifications through too many different mediums).

- Connection problems or technology glitches. This might lead to response delays or problems with individuals being unable to contribute.

- Lack of team cohesion or trust, where remote relationships are not fully established.

- Ineffective virtual meetings. This could be as a result of a lack of meeting etiquette, technology skills or having too many people in attendance.

In a hybrid team, there is a potential for an imbalance in information and knowledge, with those who are in the office more often having greater access to information than others who are working more remotely regularly.

All of these challenges and risks can be addressed with deliberate strategies to ensure remote success.

Tip

Take personal responsibility for communication. In a remote team, communication needs to be a shared responsibility so be sure to play your part in this. Update people regularly and share information generously.

In remote teams, it is good practice to have locally agreed team norms for communication. These informal agreements may address issues such as what technology to use for what particular type of communication, how often to communicate and, in the context of a hybrid team, what communication will be virtual and what will be face to face. These agreements can help to reduce communication overload, improve the meeting experience and increase participation. Where these agreements do not exist, or where there are only informal understandings, this can lead to confusion or miscommunications. Remote and hybrid teams should work together to create and document effective ways of communicating for their specific context.

> **Tip**
>
> If there are no local or team agreements about communication for remote workers in your organization, suggest beginning a group discussion to create some. Consider tools and technologies, preferences, potential challenges and barriers, and responsibilities.

Asynchronous versus synchronous communication

A common communication mistake when working remotely is to focus too much on synchronous communication (such as online meetings), resulting in a lot of screen time but not a lot of thinking time. Meeting culture, and the tendency towards excessive meetings, is a very real problem in many organizations, whether people are remote or co-located.

Too many online meetings can also contribute to some of the well-being issues that will be explored in Chapter 5. Many organizations will already have both asynchronous and synchronous communication taking place – although as we have already discussed, not everyone gives enough thought to when each one *should* be used to best effect, for which type of work.

Asynchronous communication can benefit remote teams (especially those that are working globally) by allowing work to take place when it suits the individual worker. Asynchronous communication has real benefits – it can support sharing and working out load, increasing transparency across teams. The use of online message systems and chats means that those who are out of the office or working at other times can loop back easily to see what has been discussed in their absence. Its informal nature can also help to replicate some of the more casual chats that might take place in a physical workspace, helping teams to build relationships and stay connected. It also provides choice for the worker; choice about when they respond and engage, supporting autonomy, focus and work–life balance. This form of communication does, however, need to be carefully managed to avoid both platform and notification overload. Some asynchronous channels are more open and available than others. Email, for example, is largely a closed loop, only seen by those who are copied in; in contrast, a message board can be available to a whole team, or indeed a whole company if they so wish.

Effective communication can be boosted by the use of asynchronous communication. The starting point is determining when best to use it, and this will vary depending on the situation, the individuals involved and the nature of the message. The following types of communication may suit an asynchronous format, allowing individual workers to engage with it at a time that suits them:

- a weekly leader's broadcast
- updates on meeting actions or project progress
- individual comments or input into a document
- creation of a report or presentation requiring input from more than one individual
- preparation for synchronous meetings
- company briefings or general updates
- some training courses

In contrast, the following forms of communication may be more suitable for synchronous communication, where delegates can discuss, share and deliberate together:

- a virtual, discursive meeting
- an online learning and development event
- collaboration activities where in-depth discussion is required
- discussion of sensitive matters
- where there is a need to build rapport or relationships
- where speed is of the essence – for example, where a quick decision is needed

Reflect

What are you communicating in a synchronous way that you could move to an asynchronous channel? What would be the most appropriate asynchronous channel for the particular type of communication?

Asynchronous tools include:

- using the app Slack to create discussion channels
- collaborating via online whiteboard Miro
- capturing comments through virtual noticeboard Padlet
- creating an informal chat space on enterprise social network Yammer
- live-streaming leaders' updates and recording them for later watching for those who can't attend in person
- writing a blog on WordPress, Wix or Medium as a tool to share opinions and ideas
- updating documents or meeting minutes on SharePoint or MS Teams

Just as with many of the aspects of remote work that we will explore, neither asynchronous nor synchronous communication is 'best' – there is only 'best fit' for the situation. Deciding what the best tool for the particular communication task is may require some experimentation. Neither approach should be an automatic default. Discussions about which type of communication to use for what situation can form part of those local agreements between members of a remote team. Effective remote communicators will be aware of when to choose the right medium and will ensure that they use a mixture of methods fit for the circumstances.

The following considerations can help you to determine whether asynchronous or synchronous communication is best when working with a remote team:

- Do you need a timely response or immediate feedback? Synchronous communication such as an online meeting may be most appropriate – alternatively using email or a messaging platform with a clear request for a prompt response.

- Is detailed discussion of a particular issue required? Go for a synchronous approach with a rich media, such as a virtual meeting that will support conversation.

- Is idea generation required? This will also lend itself to a synchronous approach to allow discussions to build – this can be complemented by real-time tools like polls or virtual discussion boards.

- Is the communication routine? Keep this to asynchronous channels such as email, blogs or a video update.

- Are you just conveying information, such as providing a general update? Use a lean, asynchronous media like email.

- Do you need to build consensus? This may lend itself better to a real-time discussion such as a virtual meeting.

- Is this an initial communication or engagement with another individual or group? Synchronous communication is likely to help build relationships more quickly – when they are established switch to asynchronous tools.

- Is the information being communicated detailed and will it require consideration and focus? Try asynchronous methods to give people time to digest and reflect on the information. This can then be followed up with either synchronous or asynchronous opportunities to discuss and respond.

- Will the communication generate questions that need to be responded to? Here, either approach can work; either a virtual meeting or online chat could provide the necessary additional information.

Remember that both asynchronous and synchronous communication can take place in person or virtually.

Effective virtual meetings

If there is one aspect of traditional office work that is much maligned by almost everyone, it is probably the meeting. 'That meeting could have been an email' is a common internet joke. Virtual meetings have their own particular challenges. Perhaps the most obvious challenge is that it is difficult to have a spontaneous meeting or a very brief discussion without at least some degree of coordination, messaging or calendar checking!

Multitasking in virtual meetings is all too common, with participants appearing present but undertaking other work at the same time. Collaboration online is not impossible but can be more difficult to manage, and may require a skilled facilitator. Excessive online meetings (both in terms of total number of meetings but also duration of them) can also lead to fatigue. When there are a lot of people in a virtual meeting it can also be difficult for everyone to get their voice heard. Getting virtual meetings right, both as an attendee and a host, is a key skill for remote work success. As with any work meeting, it's not about how often you meet but how valuable and useful those interactions are for the people attending them.

There are two forms of online meeting: one in which every participant is remote and attending virtually; and a hybrid meeting, where some attendees join in person (usually in the office) and others join online. The latter can be particularly challenging, especially in terms of ensuring that everyone has an equal opportunity to contribute. Remote participants can often feel like it is harder to get their voice heard and the meeting often results in something known as 'presence disparity', which refers to how those present physically in the meeting have a different (usually better) experience of it than those who are attending virtually. Depending on the nature of the discussions or the purpose of the meeting, it may actually be better to avoid this form of meeting altogether.

Tip

If a hybrid meeting cannot be avoided, take deliberate steps to bring everyone into the conversation and make sure that those attending remotely aren't forgotten or left out. Go around the virtual room in turn, inviting each individual to share their perspectives.

TOP TIPS
Running hybrid meetings

- Don't allow discussions to begin before the meeting, such as while people are arriving or getting coffee – otherwise this will exclude those who are joining remotely at the allotted time. Also ensure that discussions do not continue after remote participants have left the 'room'.

- Make sure that in-person participants don't have side conversations that remote attendees cannot hear or participate in. This will also lead to remote attendees feeling excluded from the conversation.

- Don't present or use other visual aids (such as flip charts or whiteboards) that remote participants cannot see properly or contribute to. If a presentation is required, or any form of collaborative activity such as writing on post-it notes or voting, use a technology solution that everyone can contribute to equally.

- Include remote participants throughout the meeting – don't wait until the end of the meeting to seek their views. Facilitators need to take steps to create equality in the space by encouraging interaction and participation throughout the meeting. Don't allow in-person participants to dominate the conversation.

- Try to ensure that everyone can see everyone else – this might include projecting remote participants onto larger screens or every in-person participant also using a laptop and joining the online space.

- Give everyone space to contribute their opinions, if necessary by going around both the physical and virtual room person by person inviting comments and contribution.

- It is advisable to keep hybrid meetings no longer than necessary, otherwise it may add to screen fatigue for the remote participants. Have regular breaks if necessary.

- Don't forget that remote participants are there!

The first step to an effective virtual meeting is determining whether a meeting is required at all. All too often the meeting is our default way of communicating, updating each other or resolving issues. There may, however, be other more effective ways to achieve the same ends. A meeting should only take place when it is the most appropriate medium for communication or discussion. Instead, for example, when the issue at hand is a routine update, consider if there is an alternative to meeting at all. Don't make the mistake of thinking that every problem, issue or discussion needs a meeting in order to make progress.

Tip

Think about whether you need a virtual meeting or is there a better way to communicate? Information exchange, general updates, review of actions or even quick decisions can be taken in online collaboration spaces. Issues that involve discussion, idea generation or collaboration may be best dealt with via a meeting.

How you can host effective virtual meetings

Where a meeting *is* required, when organizing or facilitating them aim to keep them as short and focused as possible to aid concentration. Remote workers will benefit by having a reputation for holding well-run, professional virtual meetings.

First of all, consider setting some meeting ground rules. Virtual meetings can make it easy to multitask – so ask people to give their full focus. This will be easier if the meeting is well run and time bound. When participants don't already know each other run a round of introductions or, where appropriate, consider a short icebreaker exercise.

Try to build rapport quickly, by using an icebreaker if appropriate, creating space for an informal chat or making a point to personally connect before jumping straight into the agenda.

Always explain at the outset of the meeting how people can contribute to the discussion: are you using chat functions, raised hands or can they simply unmute and ask a question? The more attendees in the meeting the greater the structure required around contributions. Every meeting should always have an agenda and a clear purpose: is the meeting to share information, make a decision or to collaborate and discuss? Participants should know why they are there. Test any technology that you are planning to use in advance of delegates arriving. Try to finish a few minutes before the meeting is due to end, as this gives people time to take a short break if they are moving onto another meeting.

Tip

Try scheduling meetings to begin at five past the hour or finish five minutes before the next hour – or schedule meetings for 45 minutes. Not every meeting needs to be an hour – but if you schedule them for an hour they will probably take that long!

EXERCISE
Running online meetings

Start an online meeting with a brief and informal check-in by encouraging a personal reflection; go round the virtual meeting room and ask everyone to take a turn. Remember that people may appear in a different order to each viewer so as a facilitator you should ask each person by name to participate. The request could be a simple 'how are you today' or why not try a positive round with each person taking turns to share a positive thing from their day or week. 'Rounds', as suggested by Nancy Kline's book *Time to Think* (1999), can help to break the ice in a meeting, build relationships and trust, and encourage thinking.
In a remote environment they can also help to bring everyone into the conversation.

Finally, if a remote team is working across multiple time zones avoid having a set time for regular meetings, especially if this means that meetings are very early or very late in the working day for some remote attendees. It is easy to default to a time that suits the majority, but changing meeting times will make it fair for all. Agree a rotating schedule of meeting times that mean that everyone has a reasonable meeting time that works for them.

Tip

Encourage meeting attendees to have their camera switched on for virtual meetings unless they have a very good reason not to. This will make it easier to build relationships and have meaningful dialogue. It is hard to build relationships with people that you cannot see.

How you can participate effectively in remote meetings

Participants in remote meetings should generally keep their camera on; as we will discuss in Chapter 6 it is important to be seen in meetings even when not actively participating. Always resist the temptation to multitask; it is often more obvious than we might think, especially if it becomes apparent when a participant is called upon to contribute. Multitasking is a myth; instead of doing two things at once we are actually repeatedly switching our focus between the two tasks, which is cognitively ineffective. When in a remote meeting, focus on the meeting.

Consider some of these tips for effective virtual meeting participation:

- Show up, completely. Be fully present and visible.
- Regularly look at the camera, not people on the screen (or yourself). While this feels somewhat unnatural, it is the best way to make eye contact with other meeting participants from their perspective.
- Make sure to use your mute function when not speaking. No one wants to hear your background noise!
- Frame yourself well. Ideally you want to appear in the centre of your screen. Make sure that you can be fully seen.
- Your background should be professional. Aim for it to be simple and uncluttered. Use virtual or blurred backgrounds if necessary to present a professional image.

Body language

When we are working remotely body language is naturally reduced. Through our screens we can only present part of our selves and see the same of others. In large virtual meetings this is particularly problematic as participants are reduced to a tiny square on the screen. This is a problem because we know that a significant amount of our communication is not just what is said but how it is said, including gestures, tone of voice and non-verbal signals, and even personal space and positioning. These actions are part of the message itself and influence how it is received and understood.

We need to take care in our remote communications in order to reduce the potential for miscommunication and make up for those missing non-verbal cues. There might also be delays or technical glitches to work around too, creating gaps in the conversation or unnatural pauses.

A great deal has been written about body language, but there are no definite explanations for any particular non-verbal signal. For example, one person's folded arms might indicate defensiveness, but another person might simply be cold. So while we should avoid making too many assumptions about people's body language, it is something that the remote worker cannot neglect.

To ensure remote success we need to focus on two elements of body language: paying attention to the body language of others and how we use our own body language effectively to support communication and relationships.

Managing your own body language

In virtual meetings it is important to consider the impact of our own body language. For example, if we are perceived to be multitasking we may inadvertently send a signal that we are disinterested or disengaged. Managing body language is often simply about being mindful of the signals we are sending – whether we intend to do so or not – and being aware too of how they may be misinterpreted. We may also need to over-emphasize our body language to ensure that it is 'heard' by others, such as increasing the gestures that we use over and above those we would use in an in-person environment.

Consider some of the following:

- Try to avoid being distracted by your own image, which is tempting in a virtual meeting.

- Balance eye contact with looking at others. To look like we are making eye contact we have to look at the camera. So although this is good in some circumstances (like presenting or interviews) it might mean that we miss subtle signals from others, so make sure to mix this with looking at others as they speak and engage.

- Take care with your posture. Slumping or leaning away may be interpreted as signals of disinterest or boredom, even if this is not the case.

- Frame yourself well in the screen. Be clearly visible to allow for eye contact and your facial and hand gestures to be seen.

- Indicate you are listening through nodding, leaning forward or using real or virtual gestures (such as emoji) to indicate your opinion.

- Think about what you wear. Although many people opt for comfort when working from home, clothes are part of body language and do send signals to others. Only some clothes will be visible, so make those count – even if what can't be seen is much more casual!

- Avoid fiddling with pens, hair or items on your desk. It can be distracting for other meeting participants, and may also signal disinterest.

- Be conscious of your facial signals and the messages that they might send. When you are speaking it will be one of the things that people notice about you most, unlike in an in-person environment where more of you will be visible. When unguarded these (as well as our posture) can 'leak' signalling subconscious thoughts.

- Watch your pace. Try not to speak too quickly and avoid jargon that might not be understood. This can have a negative impact on the extent to which people can understand your points.

- If you are the facilitator or the most senior person in the meeting, be aware of the shadow of your body language. What you allow will continue. For example, if you appear not to be paying attention or turn your camera off, this will signal what is acceptable and others will quickly follow suit.

Understanding the body language of others

There are no certainties with body language and it is important to avoid assumptions, especially in a remote environment where we only have part of the picture. For example, someone might not look like they are paying attention but they could simply be looking at a second screen. It is perhaps easier to misinterpret body language when working virtually.

In terms of understanding the body language of others, be alert for signs, especially weaker signals, that another person with whom you are working online is not understanding, is distracted, unhappy or disengaged. It may or may not be appropriate to call that out depending on the nature of the meeting. Either pause and invite questions or comments, or take the time to check in with the individual at a later point.

Presenting online

Hosting remote meetings can often require a presentation or use of visual materials. Developing and delivering engaging presentations is a specific communication skill that all professionals need to learn. All the typically good practice elements of effective presentations still apply in a remote environment; however, special consideration has to be given to a few key issues. Participants may be viewing the presentation on different-sized screens, they may be experiencing online meeting fatigue and body language (part of the message) is reduced. The image of the presenter may be very small in comparison to an in-person presentation. You are unlikely to be able to see the reactions of the delegates and feedback is reduced or needs to be managed through the technology which can make for a more stilted experience. Finally there is always the potential for technological glitches to contend with.

The presentation material itself is key to creating a good presentation experience. In-person presentation best practice applies here too. When using slides, less is always more. Slides, and the content within them, should be kept to a minimum to avoid creating online fatigue in attendees. Online meetings platforms have a variety of different tools to encourage interaction, from polls to virtual whiteboards. These can be useful for maintaining engagement and encouraging feedback; do, however, use these with care as overuse can be distracting. When using slides you should:

- Avoid including too much material on each slide, including text effects or too many images. These will distract from the message.

- Remember that they are not the entire presentation even when presenting online – the presenter is. The slides are a visual aid only to illustrate key points.

- Include key takeaways and two or three key points on the slides – not the entire message.

- Use simple images (take care with copyright) to illustrate points rather than text.

- Remember the old adage: tell them what you are going to tell them, tell them, then tell them what you told them.

- Be mindful of font size. Don't use anything that is too small for the audience to see well. If you have to reduce the font size to fit everything in, you might just be trying to put too much on your slide.

- Ask delegates to turn on speaker view rather than gallery view or where available use spotlight features. They will then highlight the presenter rather than the entire room of attendees.

Consider the following tips for effective online presentations:

- Frame yourself well in the screen so that your image is as visible as possible even if it is appearing in a small section of the delegate view.

- Turn off any other notifications such as email so that no additional sound can be heard by the audience.

- Don't be the person who can't share the slides properly! Always make sure you know what system you are using to present and practise if necessary to ensure you can create a seamless experience. If you are presenting via an external system (such as at an online conference) ask for a practice session to check everything works.

- Work on your tone of voice and eye contact to compensate for your lack of body language. Try to make it engaging and interesting. Avoid reading from a script, practising in advance where necessary. Look at the camera, not yourself.

- Manage the method for contribution. If you are happy for chat to take place while you are presenting (and this will not distract you) say so. Otherwise consider disabling it if the system allows. Advise the audience whether they should ask questions throughout or wait until the end of the presentation, and confirm how they should do this. If there are more than 20 attendees this is better managed through a chat or 'raised hands' function.

- Don't make the presentation any longer than it needs to be. If appropriate send pre-reading to reduce the length. Aim for no more than 20–25 minutes to avoid attendees becoming distracted.

- Involve the audience by using quick polls, questions or reactions. This will increase engagement and attention.

- Let your passion and interest in your topic do some of the talking – not just your slides.

Think carefully about whether or not you want to record your presentations. This is a common request in the virtual world – and there are both upsides and downsides. If people know there is a recording they may not turn up on the day, intending to watch it later – but may not actually get round to doing so. This also reduces the opportunity for dialogue, making the presentation truly one way. Having a 'live' event only will encourage people to attend, but this may in turn limit some people's opportunity to attend if they are, for example, working in different time zones.

- Which technology platform do we want to use for our meetings?

- What technology platform do we want to use for asynchronous team communication?

- How should we deal with general or status updates?

- What barriers to great communication might we have in our team, and how can we overcome these?

- What are our personal responsibilities for effective team communication?

- How will we record information and where do we share it (for example, minutes or actions)?

- If we have a hybrid meeting, how can we ensure a consistent experience for all attendees, whether they are attending in person or remotely?

- How can we ensure that our communication choices are consistent with well-being and work–life balance?

Work through the answers to these questions, making a note of what has been agreed. Remember to review your communication agreements or principles periodically to make sure that they are still working effectively. Don't forget to share your communication agreements with any new starters to the team.

Summary points

- Digital communication can increase significantly when remote working, both in volume and complexity. Digital communication (in excess) can also lead to fatigue due to excessive screen time.

- Hybrid work brings additional communication challenges as those undertaking hybrid work will be working in different locations, with teams working a mix of co-located and remote work.

- When communicating as a remote worker there is a need to determine the most appropriate medium for any particular message; this will involve considering the nature of the message, its complexity, urgency and what you expect from people in response.

- Remote and hybrid meetings need to be managed with care and focus to ensure that they deliver as a useful method of communication. They should not be a default method for communicating – but used when it is the most appropriate medium for the message.

- Remote communication involves more technology and fewer non-verbal cues – these make up a significant part of how we communicate so we need to adjust our approach to take this into account.

- In remote and hybrid teams, everyone needs to take responsibility for effective communication. This may involve the need to create shared norms and local ways of working.

- When working remotely it is essential to communicate with care: think about the medium and the message. Consider where misunderstandings could arise and aim to prevent them. Aim for clarity in every communication.

05

Your well-being as a remote or hybrid worker

In Chapter 2 we explored some of the challenges of working remotely. Well-being can be one of these very real challenges, and the complexities of remote working and well-being demands detailed discussion. Although remote work does bring its challenges, well-being can be enhanced through remote work too.

Well-being is a very personal issue; what supports your well-being will detract from someone else's. Some people will thrive when working remotely or from home; for other people it is much more difficult. This chapter will discuss the main challenges and some potential solutions. However, not everything will amount to a challenge for every remote or home worker. Every remote worker should take the time to reflect on how their well-being is influenced by remote work (whether positively or negatively) and what particular strategies they can employ to maximize its benefits or address its challenges.

Well-being challenges of remote work

Work extensification

First of all, working from home can lead to you having a longer working day. Some people will find themselves working the hours that they would have spent commuting, starting earlier and finishing later than their contractual working hours. Others will feel that they have to work longer to somehow prove that they are working or are just as dedicated as colleagues who may be in the office; this is often driven by fear or guilt. This is known as digital presenteeism – employees being constantly present online because they believe that they need to be seen, regardless of whether they are being effective. Sometimes it is simply easy to fall into a habit of continuing to work because work equipment is there in the home, with no commute to force a stop time.

Work–life balance

Work–life balance is a broad term used to describe how we manage the different parts of our lives, whether that is work or non-work activities. There are many definitions of work–life balance, but it typically refers to a situation where people have achieved their own personal, effective state of balance between their work and other non-work aspects of their life. However work–life balance is defined, it is a very personal concept: what supports or detracts from personal balance will vary significantly from person to person and from situation to situation.

Working from home can lead to a particular work–life balance change – something that is often described as blurred boundaries. This refers to a lack of segmentation between the work and home aspects of a remote worker's life. Work (and work equipment) is always present, making it difficult to switch off. For some people this is not a problem, and they are quite comfortable switching between work and home tasks or when one sphere intrudes on another. For others, this is a considerable source of stress. Work–life balance research differentiates broadly between two types of people: integrators (comfortable with switching between work and non-work tasks and blurred boundaries) and separators (people who need strong boundaries between the two). For example, if an integrator was working from home and a family member came into their office to discuss a home issue, this wouldn't necessarily cause them a problem and they would find it easy to switch back to the work task again afterwards. A separator might find the interruption more challenging, or it might take them time to refocus again on work. People with high separation needs may simply not be suited to working from home unless they are able to establish those boundaries in an achievable way.

It isn't necessarily better to be an integrator rather than a separator – but a tendency towards one or the other might result in the need to deploy different strategies. For example, the integrators' comfort with having their work and home life combined might lead them to work on holidays or at the weekends. If they don't have good boundaries in place they might find themselves overworking or creating conflict at home. The natural separator needs that clear line between work and home, although this for some feels difficult to obtain, especially in constantly connected culture.

People who identify closely with needing separation must give greater consideration to how working from home can work for them. It is inevitable when working from home that there will be some spill-over from work to home and vice versa, and total separation may be difficult to achieve. Separators should therefore reflect on how they could get a little more comfortable with integration, in a way that is manageable for them, or how they might develop appropriate strategies for coping with 'overspill' of work into home.

Reflect

What is your working style? Would you consider yourself to be more of an integrator, or a separator? What does this mean for your remote work routine?

Everyone has different work–life balance needs. Some people don't actually like the term 'work–life balance' because it implies that an equal balance can (or indeed should) be achieved, when in reality there is more likely to be an ebb and flow. There will be times that our work life dominates, and other times when family takes precedence. Those who dislike the idea of work–life balance believe we should instead look towards being comfortable with integration. After all, we are all one person, made up of the work self and the non-work self.

The very personal nature of both working styles and preferences combined with the equally personal nature of health and well-being mean that there can be no simple advice or guidance that can apply to everyone in all circumstances. Instead, the remote or hybrid worker should reflect on their own style, how to put in appropriate strategies for that style, and importantly, how to communicate style and preferences to others.

Reflect

Who do you need to talk to about your working style and work–life balance needs? What do you need to share with them, or ask of them?

Isolation

Remote work can also be quite lonely, and sometimes you may feel isolated from your colleagues. Part of work, and many workplaces, is social connection. Time with others is a known enabler of well-being. Those crucial support systems that arise in offices may not easily be replicated at home. The impact of this will vary from person to person: some will thrive on the quiet and solitude; others will find it a bigger challenge.

Tip

If you are working remotely and feel that you are missing out on interactions with others, why not consider using co-working spaces or hubs? These are becoming increasingly common, and provide the option to rent a regular space or just use a meeting room for a day or few hours.

Digital well-being

The technology that we use every day to undertake remote work can have an impact on our mental, physical and emotional health. This may relate to the technology itself or its excess use.

During the Covid-19 pandemic businesses rushed to introduce online meeting systems. Although they were not by any means new, they weren't necessarily commonplace in many organizations and employees had to learn new skills at speed. Those online meetings proliferated, and a new term soon entered our language: 'Zoom Fatigue'. Not just related to that particular meeting platform, this was a shorthand to describe the tiredness that can result from spending long periods in online meetings. Research from Stanford University looked at just why we find online meetings so tiring (Ramachandran, 2021). They found that there is a higher cognitive load from these meetings, including the unnatural act of looking at our own image for long periods. Combine this with the number of different digital technologies that we are using, and through which we are constantly connected, and we have a recipe for exhaustion.

Too much time on devices, especially late at night, can disrupt sleep, as the blue light emitted can have a negative impact on our natural sleep cycles by delaying the release of sleep-inducing melatonin and by increasing our alertness. Too many notifications from multiple digital channels can lead to 'technoference', where technology interrupts daily life, interrupting focus and productivity. Any of these issues can impact upon the remote worker as so much of their work is undertaken through digital tools. It is therefore important for remote or hybrid workers to be aware of the positives and negatives of tech on well-being, using digital tools positively and effectively managing their digital workload.

Tip

To reduce eye strain, take a 20-second break from the screen every 20 minutes, and focus on something that is 20 feet away. Remember: 20, 20, 20!

> **Tip**
>
> If you are a remote or hybrid worker and you are unwell be sure to take sick leave. It is all too easy to carry on working when you are based at home. However, this might delay your recovery and if you are in a position of seniority or influence, encourage others to work when unwell too.

Transition

When we work in an office, our home and work spaces are entirely separate, and our commute provides a transition between the two. Commutes may be long or short, expensive or cheap, involve public transport or not. The commute is not, however, just about the travel to and from work itself. It also fulfils a function: it provides a space between work lives and home lives. This is often referred to as a 'transition'.

This transition is essentially a gap in which we move not just physically but also mentally from one part of our life to another. We can transition from our work selves to our home selves – something that some people need more than others. In that sense the commute has a purpose beyond simply moving from place to place. Some people use their commute to do work tasks. Others use it for non-work activities like reading or listening to music. Even when people work while commuting, they are still moving away from their normal workspace and all that it entails.

In the home working environment this transition is absent, and may amount to no more than shutting a laptop screen. When we work from home our work equipment is often more visible. Not everyone will have a separate workspace, and it becomes all too easy to spend a lot more time working, checking our emails or responding to one last message. With no train or bus to catch, there is simply nothing to stop us working. These blurred boundaries can also lead to work–life conflict. This is where work demands can spill over into family life or vice versa, causing stress or interference.

Reflect

How well do you balance the work and non-work aspects of your life? Do you actively manage your boundaries? Do you need to create any specific transition rituals?

Well-being benefits of remote work

In direct contrast to the challenges described above, remote working can also bring potential benefits to individuals too. Some studies have found that employees who work remotely can have greater job satisfaction and experience less stress than their office-based counterparts.

One of the main well-being benefits associated with remote work is a reduced or entirely absent commute. Long commutes are associated with reduced life satisfaction and can be a cause of stress, especially when the commute involves public transport (people who use buses and trains to get to work report the greatest negative impact on their lives). Working remotely can allow people to use former commuting time in a way that supports or improves their physical or psychological health and well-being such as time with friends and family, or for exercise or hobbies. Unfortunately, when people work remotely, especially from home, they don't always reap these benefits, as we have discussed.

Remote work also can allow for greater personalization of work, especially around personal energies and our circadian rhythms. When we work in an office, we tend to default for the most part to an eight-hour working day. This usually involves working for three or four hours, a lunchbreak, and then a similar additional period of work. However, when it comes to energy (and indeed how we recover from the energy we expend while working) we are not all the same. Some of us will be morning people, others more effective late in the evening. Some people will work better in short bursts with more regular breaks. When working remotely we are no longer required (assuming our employer does not demand the office structure is replicated) to work in the same way as we would in a physical location. This can support our overall personal productivity.

As demonstrated here, the relationship between remote and home working and well-being is complex. Successful remote workers therefore need strategies for managing work–life balance, managing the boundaries between work and home (even if they are the same place), and coping with digital overload. When workers are proactive and take steps to mitigate the potential downsides of remote work, well-being overall can improve.

Reflect

Does working remotely currently enhance or detract from your well-being? What strategies do you need to employ to ensure working remotely delivers maximum well-being opportunities?

Managing your well-being when working remotely

When working remotely, the aim should be 'thriving' not merely surviving. Well-being is a highly personal construct – and it begins with self-awareness. The following steps can support individuals in enabling their well-being when working from home, as well as mitigating some of the potential pitfalls. Some of these examples are practical and others amount to what is known as 'boundary management'. This term refers to techniques used to identify and manage the boundaries between work and home, or other non-work activities. Effective boundary management can help individuals to find a healthy work–life balance. Some people will need more boundaries than others depending on their personal working preferences.

First of all, workstations need to be properly set up to support comfortable and safe working. Wherever possible, workstations should be near a source of natural daylight with minimal clutter, as excess clutter in the working environment has been found to create a stress response.

The next step is to create a separate place for your work in your home if possible. This will allow some physical separation between work and non-work activities. Ideally, work tasks will take place in a separate room, but this won't be an option for everyone. An alternative is to put away all work equipment at the end of the working day where it is out of sight, helping to create a boundary and reduce the temptation to check one more email. Even a box or a drawer will suffice.

Another way to address the issue of blurred boundaries between work and home is to replicate the transition period that is usually provided by a commute. This provides a gap between work and non-work activities and can help create a sense that work has ended. There are many ways to achieve this. Some people go for a short walk before or after the work day is completed. Others create a ritual that performs the same function; something as simple as making a cup of tea, playing some music or changing clothes can also provide a mental transition, and so can moving into a different space in the house from where work takes place. There's no need to create an elaborate ritual – simply create a personal contrast between work and non-work.

It is all too easy when working from home to skip lunch, spend the whole day sitting down or staring at a screen. To offset the sedentary nature of working from home, a standing desk that allows a choice between sitting and standing will help to bring movement into the working day. Movement can also be introduced through regular stretching and taking breaks throughout the working day. Eyes need a break just as much as brains do. Wherever possible, short gaps should be scheduled between meetings to facilitate movement and reduce screen time. Breaks between meetings allow the brain to re-set. If necessary, using timers or other reminders that it is time to take a break can help – there are even remote working apps designed to do just this. Recognize the importance of stepping away from the desk. Time away from both desk and screen should be considered an essential part of the working day.

At the end of the working day it is also important to meaningfully disconnect from work devices and to ensure work truly stops. Hybrid work should not mean that employees are 'always on'. This might include turning off email or other message notifications, or during weekend or holiday periods using auto-email responses that advise that messages are not being monitored and when a response can be expected – and sticking to this. Too often people use 'out of office' messages but monitor their inboxes and respond anyway, creating a future expectation that a response will follow and that disturbing holidays is acceptable. The following tips may also help to ensure digital well-being by managing notifications or reducing use:

- mute notifications and chats, use focus mode or turn off vibrations
- simplify the home screens on mobile devices, or delete unused apps
- monitor usage on mobile devices or use usage reminders
- create a device-free time or zone in the home
- go back to paper – use a notebook or pen and paper for notes or to-do lists

Some people will benefit from a structured routine and set working hours to prevent them from overworking. For others this might be too rigid, reducing the sense of autonomy and choice. There is no single right way to switch off and manage working hours; remote workers may need to spend some time experimenting with different solutions to find the one that works for them. Examples of healthy work–life boundaries include:

- setting a dedicated stop time
- not checking emails at the weekend or after a specific time in the evening

- muting notifications during family time
- a 'no phones' rule during meal times
- not accepting meeting requests at certain times
- blocking out break times in a work diary

Finally, to reduce loneliness or the sense of isolation that can arise from remote work, workers need to intentionally reach out to colleagues to create those social connections and build relationships. Connecting with others has been found to support and enable personal well-being.

EXERCISE
Improving well-being

Reflect on the challenges of remote work set out earlier in this chapter. Which of these are *your* personal challenges, or where might you have the potential to experience difficulties?

Identify which of the steps to improve well-being might be the most appropriate for you to take to ensure that you are working with your own well-being in mind. Commit to taking these steps, making a plan of action where necessary. Is there anyone you need to share this plan with?

Summary points

- Remote and hybrid work can benefit individual well-being – or detract from it. The latter can happen when remote work is poorly implemented, when there is an unhealthy organizational culture surrounding remote work, or when individual remote workers do not establish healthy working practices.

- There is a great deal of good practice advice on well-being and remote work. Well-being and work–life balance are, however, very personal concepts. Each remote worker will need to reflect on their own preferences, working styles and needs in order to establish what works for them, and then put actions in place. Self-care starts with self-awareness.

- Remote workers need to employ personally tailored strategies and approaches to ensure that remote work helps them to thrive, contributing positively to work–life balance and health.

06
Your presence and personal brand

A lack of visibility at work can be problematic. Research suggests that we are influenced by seeing people work, even if we don't actually know what they are doing. This effect can be especially enhanced when we see people working long hours.

This can present a particular challenge for remote workers: how can they make sure that not only are they successfully delivering and meeting our performance targets, but that people are also aware that they are? Unfortunately, flexible and remote work can be associated with 'flexible working stigma'. This refers to a particular kind of bias that is experienced by flexible workers, where they are assumed to be somehow less committed to their job or organization, resulting in negative career outcomes around progression, recognition and reward. Another challenge related to remote work is confidence; not everyone finds it easy to speak up or to assert themselves in a remote environment. This might be particularly problematic for naturally quieter or more introverted individuals, especially when remote meetings are not well facilitated, making it difficult to be heard.

Taking a proactive and focused approach to your personal branding and presence is part of the solution to the challenges of remote work visibility and is key to building a strong personal reputation. Arguably, all employees should consider their personal brands in a planned way, especially in an age of social media where a wealth of information can exist about individuals online. Through personal branding, this online information can be consciously managed – but also made to work effectively in support of relationship building and career development.

Your visibility

Visibility is quite simply about being seen and contributing in a noticeable way. Visibility when working remotely can be enhanced by speaking up and aiming to stand out. Not everyone finds this easy or natural, and it can require some practice. It is possible to be seen and build visibility in both online spaces and face to face.

Online visibility can be achieved through clearly signalling working hours and availability, through auto-signatures or signals on collaboration systems (such as the 'colour' on Microsoft Teams that indicates online status). Joining in online discussions, contributing ideas and asking questions in meetings are all simple ways to build visibility – wherever and whenever work takes place.

From a career perspective, remote workers need to ensure that 'out of sight' does not mean 'out of mind' – specifically that working remotely does not lead to fewer career and development opportunities. This is especially important when an organization (or an individual manager) is not fully committed to supporting remote work.

When we work remotely we are often predominantly visible only through a small screen. Being seen can be challenging, and more difficult to achieve than in face-to-face environments. One way that we can build visibility is to place deliberate focus on building personal relationships and networking internally. We tend to think of professional networking as something that we do externally at events or on specialist social media platforms like LinkedIn. It is, however, just as important to network internally too. Future success and career opportunities can depend on being noticed by the right people. Tips on building professional networks can be found in Chapter 7 on career management.

Another way to enhance visibility is for remote workers to put themselves forward for opportunities or get involved in groups. This doesn't necessarily have to mean work-related projects; it could be joining a club (or setting one up if they don't exist – lots of organizations have online book clubs or virtual exercise groups) or arranging a social activity.

Tip

Before attending a meeting, review the agenda or any pre-reading, and prepare some thoughtful questions in advance that you can ask in the meeting or post in a virtual chat. This will help to support your visibility.

In many ways we would hope that our work and efforts will speak for themselves. Unfortunately, this is not always the case. Instead, it is important to signal what we do, through being seen working (even if this is demonstrated virtually) or through focusing on building 'face time' with colleagues and managers. This is especially important for new starters who have less well-established relationships in the organization. Signalling also refers to the idea that an employee needs to signal to colleagues and their manager that they have desirable skills and behaviours. For example, in an office environment an individual can signal that they have good time management through being punctual. In a remote environment it's unlikely that people will see what time they start work each day – but we can instead signal our time management skills through being punctual for online meetings or delivering our work on time. This does of course need to be balanced with well-being; signalling too much availability (such as being available at all hours of the day) might lead to overwork.

Reflect

How visible are you in your current role? How can you be more visible? To whom do you need to be visible?

Some fully remote organizations do provide occasional opportunities for teams (or even the whole company) to meet up for events or conferences. Where these are available, the remote worker should maximize the opportunity to build visibility in person, to complement their more regular virtual efforts. Treat them as a chance to turbo-charge existing relationships as well as create brand new ones.

Tip

Hybrid workers have the opportunity to get face time during their office-based days – an advantage over fully remote colleagues. Hybrid workers therefore should be sure to make the most of these opportunities, focusing on visibility and connecting during this time, rather than on solo tasks.

Your personal brand

Personal branding refers to the process of deliberately managing your personal reputation and self-promotion. The concept of personal branding was first introduced in 1997 by leading management thinker Tom Peters, who believed that individuals should borrow from traditional corporate marketing concepts when promoting themselves – defining what makes them unique, their own personal set of skills, experiences and knowledge in order to differentiate. Together these elements can be described as a 'personal value proposition' – another term that we know from marketing theory.

Personal brand is often informally described as 'what people say about you when you are not in the room'. A personal brand can be developed by anyone, starting with the process of considering what they would like to be known for and what unique strengths they possess. Essentially, your personal brand is your professional reputation. Everyone has a personal brand – but not everyone is taking a planned approach to its management and development. Doing so can be beneficial to any professional, but becomes even more critical for the remote or hybrid worker as it will help to offset the natural reduced visibility of remote work.

Reflect

What do you think people currently say about you when you are not in the room? What would you like them to say?

Consider some of these tips for reflecting on and building personal brand:

- What are your skills, experiences, abilities or strengths?
- What have you accomplished, or what are you proud of?
- What makes you different? What can you do that other people cannot?
- What do you want to be known for?
- How can you influence how you are perceived?
- How can you promote your skills and achievements and let people know about your strengths and skills?
- How can you portray a professional image in the workplace?

EXERCISE
Creating your elevator pitch

One way to reinforce personal brand is to have what is often referred to as an 'elevator pitch', so called as it demands you are able to introduce yourself effectively and memorably in the time it takes to go from one floor to another in an elevator (or lift!).

Having a concise but powerful personal introduction is a useful exercise, and can help to ensure any opportunity to introduce yourself while working remotely is fully maximized. Draft and practise a powerful introduction to you.

As a remote and hybrid worker you should ensure that you are making the most of your time in the office or with others to increase your visibility or enhance a personal brand. When working remotely, reputation and personal brand need to be built at a distance. Individuals need to demonstrate their value in a different way. Ideally we want our colleagues to form positive perceptions of us, and we may therefore need to employ influencing skills to achieve this, in conjunction with demonstrating our interpersonal skills.

Influencing encompasses many things and employs a mixture of different personal skills. Influencing is generally considered to be the ability to affect the way that people think, act or behave as a result of our own behaviour and actions. It isn't about using power inappropriately or trying to force people to agree with us, but rather positively persuading or inspiring change. The ability to influence can come from different places: it may be because we have actual power through a position that we hold; it may come from the fact that we have access to certain information; or because we have a particular expertise that others do not. Some people are able to influence through their personality, because they are likeable, charismatic or demonstrate certain attractive traits. Visibility and influence are linked; unless we are visible, unless we have the necessary, established personal relationships it will be difficult to influence others. Influence is also linked to trust, discussed below.

How can we therefore build our influence with others, in order to support our remote work success? Dr Robert Cialdini is an expert on the subject, and has distilled these abilities to influence and persuade others into six core principles: reciprocity, scarcity, authority, commitment and consistency, likeability, and consensus (Cialdini, 2006). Of these six, two are particularly relevant here: likeability and reciprocity. Quite simply, we are influenced by, and trust and build relationships with, people that we find likeable; they will be influenced by us in return if they find us likeable too. Another one of his principles is reciprocity; when we do something for people they are more likely to treat us in the same way and do something back in return. Cialdini believes that these two elements overlap; they are both relationship-based. There are also overlaps between the skills of influencing and the skills of good communication: listening, emotional intelligence and communication. We can influence people positively through how we behave and how we show up at work. We can influence them when we are trusted, credible and collaborative. These factors in turn support likeability – we have a positive reinforcing circle of supporting behaviours which are also closely linked to those same skills that facilitate good remote work. In summary: focus on the skills discussed in Chapter 1 and these will naturally help you to build your visibility, influence and personal brand.

Reflect

Consider some of the following:

- Who do you need to influence at work?
- About what do you need to influence others?
- How effective are your influencing skills, and where do you develop?

Trust

In many ways, remote work is built on trust. Managers have to trust their teams to work without close supervision, and teams have to trust each other too. High trust environments lead to positive organizational outcomes. They are also psychologically safe, meaning that people will feel that it is acceptable to speak up, to be themselves and to challenge. For remote workers themselves, it is important to be seen as trusted individuals. This is just one more facet of a desirable remote reputation, going to the heart of the personal brand. For those not yet working remotely but who would like to do so, a trusted reputation can be the key to unlocking the opportunity. Managers often worry about whether someone will perform effectively when working remotely without supervision, although there is no evidence to suggest that this is a common problem.

There are lots of different ways in which we can define trust, and a range of academic and leadership models that discuss it from an organizational perspective. At an individual level, trust is about being dependable, consistent, transparent and reliable.

There are a number of behaviours that you can demonstrate in order to signal your trustworthiness:

- doing what you say you will do
- delivering on time
- taking time to get to know others on a personal level
- demonstrating empathy
- showing trust towards others
- collaborating and communicating with others
- demonstrating competence in role

In an ideal world, trust would arise naturally and quickly. However, this does not always happen in practice. Trust often grows over time as relationships become more established and people learn that it is safe to trust. In a traditional office environment, communication and contact can be more informal and regular, and is not necessarily structured predominantly around activities or meetings.

Working relationships can therefore be established, and trust along with them, more quickly than they might in a remote environment, unless time is devoted specifically to this activity.

Trusting other people involves an element of risk; sometimes when trust is provided it will not be reciprocated or honoured. When trust is established, it can be quickly damaged too. The remote worker who wishes to be trusted (receiving the potential career benefits that this can deliver) would be advised to focus on building meaningful personal relationships with colleagues, and finding ways to signal those behaviours and competencies that identify them as trustworthy. Remote workers need to show that they are worthy of taking the risk to trust them, and that they will not breach trust placed in them. Trust can be undermined by the opposite behaviours to those described above: unreliability, inconsistency, failure to deliver or to contribute, a lack of attention to personal relationships. Remote workers must avoid these at all costs or risk derailing career success, or even their access to remote or hybrid work.

TOP TIPS
Building your presence and personal brand

- When working remotely, a more focused effort is required to build relationships and network with other people. Allocate time every week to build and nurture professional relationships.

- Always include a photograph on social media sites or any platforms (such as Zoom or Slack) that allow you to upload one. Consider using both internal and external social media platforms to connect with colleagues.

- Don't be afraid to share your successes and achievements (appropriately) with colleagues and your manager.

- Suggest meeting colleagues (virtually or in person if appropriate) for coffee so that you can learn more about their role. Most people will be more than happy to share information about what they do.

- During meetings, take time to engage in social conversations and get to know colleagues. This can be as simple as checking in and asking how people are or asking other general questions.
- Pay attention to your appearance in online meetings and avoid multitasking.
- Make use of opportunities to network with colleagues, either face to face or virtually. Join internal social networks like Yammer or Workplace and join in conversations there.
- Take (healthy) opportunities to get noticed. This is especially important for those new to an organization or role. This should not, however, translate into digital presenteeism or working excessive hours.

Summary points

- A lack of visibility at work can unfortunately result in poor career outcomes – out of sight can sometimes mean out of mind.
- By its very nature remote work can be less visible than office-based or co-located work. To ensure success therefore, remote workers need to focus deliberately on visibility, presence and their personal brand.
- Hybrid workers can take a focused approach to maximizing face time proactively with colleagues in their office-based time – supporting visibility.
- Trust is key to remote and hybrid work. Being a trusted member of the team is part of professional reputation; remote and hybrid workers can take steps to demonstrate and signal trusted behaviours.
- Visibility and personal brand management includes a degree of self-promotion and sharing success.

07
Managing your career as a remote worker

Career management can include ensuring success in a current role or working towards future progression. It is a term that refers to taking a structured and planned approach to an individual's career and professional development. Although not something that everyone necessarily undertakes, all professionals can benefit from an organized approach to their own career management.

While organizations and managers may be able to provide help and support, career management is ultimately the responsibility of the individual. The idea of the 'job for life' is long gone and no set of skills or qualifications can provide any one professional with everything they need for their entire career. Jobs, organizations and technology are continually changing – often at pace – and employees need to adapt to these changes as they arise. Active career management combined with ongoing professional development is therefore an essential for every professional – remote, hybrid or co-located.

Career management encompasses getting the right job, continuing professional development, planning for the future, enhancing skills and networking. In a remote or hybrid environment there are adaptions and evolutions of more traditional career management techniques. Some of these techniques we have already discussed, such as managing visibility and personal brand. In this chapter we will consider more traditional aspects of career management such as interviews and starting a new role.

Maybe you have concerns that working remotely can be damaging for career development. Unfortunately, there are still those who believe that people who want to work remotely are somehow less committed to their careers or interested in their work. Remote work, however, can have real advantages for some careers; in particular, the ability to work remotely can help to level the playing field for those who find it difficult to commute or work the traditional 9 to 5, such as those with caring responsibilities or disabilities.

EXERCISE
Undertaking your personal SWOT analysis

Good career management begins with self-awareness. Why not start with an audit of you?

You will probably have heard of a SWOT analysis tool (strengths, weaknesses, opportunities and threats) but you may not have thought about doing one of these evaluations on yourself. Take some time to reflect on your current strengths, development areas (weaknesses), opportunities and threats with reference to your career. While undertaking this analysis, give specific consideration to the impact of remote or hybrid work.

When it is complete you may find it helpful to discuss the review with your manager as they may be able to contribute to the review but also support you in addressing some of the development areas or opportunities.

Remote job interviews

Remote job interviews are becoming increasingly common. Some organizations run these as live virtual interviews, while others will ask candidates to record and upload videos that a recruiter can watch in their own time. Employers may build remote interviews into a process even when roles are not remote (or only partly remote/hybrid) for speed and ease, especially when they have a large volume of applicants.

There are two aspects to consider regarding the remote job interview. First of all, there are the practicalities of coming across well in a virtual environment, putting forward your best possible self. Secondly, where the job is likely to involve a significant amount of remote and hybrid work, the hiring manager may well ask questions specifically related to remote work to assess the candidate's skills and abilities.

In terms of the interview itself, all the usual good practice applies in a remote environment as it does in a face-to-face one. Being on time, undertaking appropriate preparation and research, making a good first impression and answering questions succinctly and comprehensively – all of these things remain important. There is, however, reduced body language and the possibility of technical glitches to deal with as well.

Here are a few tips for successful remote job interviews:

- Make sure that you are familiar with the technology that will be used on the day. Practise if necessary. Also, check your audio in advance where possible.

- Use eye contact. It's tempting to have notes and prompts to hand when interviewing remotely. However, while these can be a useful aid to memory, make sure not to rely too heavily on them as this will inevitably lead to reduced eye contact. Replicating eye contact in a virtual meeting is best achieved through looking at the camera, not the people on the screen.

- Make sure you have a professional screen name. Check this in advance, especially if you are using someone else's system or account to join the interview. Similarly, if there is an avatar, make sure this is professional and ideally the same one you use in your professional networking sites.

- Body language. As we have discussed in Chapter 4 on communication, body language is significantly reduced in a virtual meeting – and of course this applies to interviews too. Use your tone of voice instead to help support your communication, make good eye contact and sit upright, directly facing the camera. Watch for any negative body language like slumping or looking down.

- If you find that you get distracted by your own image, see if the software allows you to minimize or turn off your self-view (only do this in the interview if you know how to do it quickly and seamlessly).

- Have an appropriate background. Ensure it is free of clutter and distractions. Where necessary blur the background or use a professional background photograph (nothing too distracting or frivolous).

- Dress for an interview. Although it is often more acceptable to dress casually when working remotely, assume smart is best for an interview and dress as you would for a face-to-face meeting.

- Manage interruptions. Although you can't control everything when interviewing from home, be sure to tell other people in the house that you need to be undisturbed, and silence other notifications. Close windows and even leave a note on your front door asking people not to knock.

- Frame yourself. Ideally you should appear centrally in the screen, be well lit, with your head and shoulders clearly visible. No one wants to look at the top of your head – or half of it!

- Enter the virtual meeting a few minutes in advance of the scheduled interview time. Be ready in case you are admitted into the virtual room early.

- Finally – if using a laptop don't forget to make sure that it is fully charged! In case of wifi issues also be ready to switch to a hotspot or mobile device in an emergency.

Remote work interview questions

Here are just a few examples of questions that recruiters might use to assess remote working skills and competencies when hiring for a fully remote or hybrid role:

- How do you organize your day and manage your time when working remotely?
- What skills do you believe remote workers need, and how do you demonstrate them?
- Give an example of when you have successfully worked remotely or in a hybrid way.
- How do you ensure that you communicate well while working remotely?
- Give an example of when you have used a range of technologies to work effectively remotely.
- What challenges do you experience as a result of remote or hybrid work, and how do you manage these?
- What is it that you enjoy most about working remotely/why have you applied for a remote role?
- How do you manage your well-being and work–life balance while undertaking remote work?
- (For hybrid roles) How do you structure your working week to ensure that you are effective and productive?
- How do you maintain your motivation while working remotely?
- If you were successful, how would you build relationships and ensure you understand our company culture when working remotely?

These questions include a mix of competency questions (looking for specific examples from previous roles) as well as strengths-based questions (what the candidate does well or where they have potential). When answering, be honest and provide specific, detailed answers. Remember: a hiring manager is looking to ensure that a future recruit is fully capable of working remotely; candidates will need to assure them that they have the necessary skills and are able to apply them appropriately.

Tip

If you haven't worked remotely before, be sure to review the skills for remote work in Chapter 1 and think about how you can demonstrate them. If you are asked about previous remote working experience, be honest, but then explain how you would approach your first remote role to ensure success.

Starting a new role remotely

Remote workers should always make sure that their home office or workstation is ready for Day One of their new job – this will help ensure an effective start. Another important early step is to gain clarity on internal policies and procedures relating to remote work. Does the organization, or specific team, have any arrangements about remote work? This might include policies around subjects like data security or expenses, through to casual 'the way we do things in our team' information.

When starting a new role remotely it can be a challenge to get to know the organization's culture. Culture is often referred to as 'the way that things are done around here' and it includes how people work and engage with each other, how work gets done, and the shared beliefs, values and norms that exist. Assimilating culture is important and getting to know colleagues and team members is a key first step.

Joining a remote or hybrid team brings with it some specific challenges around getting to know people, building relationships and personal visibility. Hopefully, the formal induction process will support these activities, but the individual employee can take their own proactive steps to create success in a new, remote team. Whether starting a job remotely, in the office, or in a hybrid model, generally speaking the corporate induction is unlikely to be enough to ensure success. Even with a supportive manager, there will be much that the remote worker needs to do proactively for themselves.

New hybrid workers should make the most of office-based time to focus on relationships and understanding culture, saving any independent tasks (such as the compulsory e-learning or online training that is included in almost every corporate induction) for remote working time. The entirely remote worker may have to do all of their induction and getting to know their new organization from home.

Tip

Don't be afraid to let people know that you are new to the organization. Most people will be happy to help or tell you more about the work that they do.

Newly remote workers should consider some of the following to help them navigate their new workplace:

- If you haven't worked from home before, follow the guidance set out in Chapter 2 on setting yourself up for success. This should be the basis of effective remote working and will make starting a new job easier.

- Set up meetings with new colleagues and stakeholders. Ask for help in identifying the right people to talk to and meet with. Initially, meetings can be short and introductory in nature but these initial connections are important and will help to pave the way for building longer-term relationships.

- Identify any other ways to connect with colleagues. Is there a communication channel for social conversations or are there any informal online activities? Do the team meet up in person and, if so, when is the next opportunity to join?

- If a buddy or coach is not provided, ask for one. They can be a point of contact for quick questions and information.

- Proactively ask your manager for regular meetings if they have not already scheduled these. Also, ask for some objectives for your first months to help you gain necessary clarity on just what is required to be successful.

- Identify any priority training requirements, for example, in specific systems that are used for remote work or communication.

- Focus on creating the right first impression and building trust with new colleagues. Use the tips and guidance in Chapter 6 to support this.

- Talk to your manager about their preferred way to receive updates and communications from you. Tailor your approach to their working style.

- If you are going to be working in a hybrid way, plan to spend a little more time in the office in your first month than you may intend to later on. This will help to speed up the process of getting to know the organization and its culture.

- Don't be afraid to ask lots of questions. It is the best way to learn.

Finally, all remote and hybrid workers will benefit from having a formal career and learning plan with established goals and associated actions. Review the information in this chapter that discusses this in more detail.

Early-career professionals

If you are an early-career professional, especially if you're a graduate or apprentice, you may find particular challenges when working remotely for the first time. Many graduates and early-career professionals may still be living with family, potentially limiting their ability to create separate or personal workspaces. They are likely to have less general experience of work along with many of the areas in this book, such as building professional relationships, using work-based technologies or understanding and adapting to organizational cultures. They may also place a higher value on the social aspects of work than other colleagues.

Even if early-career professionals have *studied* from home, this experience does not necessarily mean that they are equipped to *work* effectively from home, as different skills are required.

Schools and universities will undoubtedly need to consider preparing current students for this future and help them to develop relevant skills. Some are already rising to the challenge, developing modules focusing on the necessary, practical skills of remote work. In the meantime, early-career professionals may wish to consider some of the following:

- Seeking out a mentor – but not their line manager – who is an experienced remote or hybrid worker.

- Undertaking any specific training opportunities provided by their employer on remote or hybrid work practice.

- Asking for support or guidance promptly if difficulties are experienced.

- Focusing on the key areas outlined in this book including relationship building, personal brand and visibility.

- Talking to their managers about how they can replace 'learning by seeing' (the type of learning undertaken by watching or listening to more experienced colleagues) with a more appropriate process fitting a hybrid working pattern.

- When working in a hybrid way, maximizing time in the workplace for relationships and understanding culture.

Building professional relationships

In Chapter 2 we discussed the importance of building effective relationships when undertaking remote work. Effective personal relationships and professional networks can also support long-term career success. Our relationships and connections can be valuable sources of learning and information and even opportunities for career development. Networking in particular is a key skill for all professionals today, supporting success in general, but also career progression. It is a cliché to say that 'it's not what you know but who you know', but this statement is to some extent based in truth. When having a career as a remote worker, building professional relationships goes beyond merely building relationships in their current workplace but wider relationships and networks too.

Much of the good practice in networking and professional relationships applies equally in a traditional or remote working environment. Being friendly and authentic, demonstrating listening skills, showing a genuine interest in people, sharing knowledge and time – these are all skills that can build both a personal network and strong business relationships – as well as being reciprocal, and a helpful member of a professional community first, rather than merely seeking to benefit from it.

When working remotely, it is easy to neglect some of the personal interactions that can support relationships, such as casual conversations before a meeting, a chat over a coffee, and even the chance meeting in a corridor. Remote workers should not overlook the importance of social connection and seek to build this in wherever possible. A simple question about someone's weekend before commencing the formal business agenda can help to create a personal connection.

In addition to the guidance provided in Chapter 2 on building virtual relationships, consider some of the following in relation to career development:

- Join relevant external networking groups or attend events by professional associations. Many of these run online events as well as in-person ones making them easily accessible. External groups can bring valuable knowledge but also address some of the isolating factors of remote work, providing an alternative professional community.

- Establish a professional-looking profile on at least one professional networking site – LinkedIn is the most popular site for professional networking. Then connect with other people in your industry. Send a polite message with your connection request that explains you are looking to build your professional network and connections. Most people will be happy to accept a request.

- Post regularly on LinkedIn or join groups there, connecting with other members appropriately. Also connect with people that you meet professionally; take the time to look them up and send them an invitation.
- Share expertise or knowledge generously within that network, connecting members to one another. As we have discussed previously when considering building influence, this creates reciprocity.
- Keep in touch with former colleagues either by connecting online or joining alumni groups.

Academic research into networking (and how information spreads across personal networks) distinguishes between strong ties and weak ties in our personal relationships. The terms are self-explanatory; strong ties refer to strong, established and often long-standing relationships, perhaps with close family, friends or colleagues. They are the people with whom we have the most frequent contact and established connections. In contrast, our weaker ties are characterized by infrequent contact or more distant relationships. In networking terms both are important. It is easy perhaps to focus on our strong ties, but it is recognized that from a career perspective weak ties are just as important. Sometimes, our strong ties are the people most like us. They will have the same knowledge and information as they do similar things and engage with the same people. Weak ties can be an important bridge to new information and ideas – and job opportunities. They know people we don't know which can also lead to further new connections.

Research undertaken at Microsoft (Longqi et al, 2021) during the early months of the Covid-19 pandemic found that when people worked from home they often found that their strong ties persisted but their weaker ties were more likely to fade away and weaken further. For example, in the office we might be on nodding terms with casual colleagues such as people in other teams, or there may be colleagues we only see occasionally such as at events or conferences.

Simply, when working remotely it is important to focus on building relationships with both strong ties (our closest colleagues) and weak ties – deliberately reaching out and connecting with a range of colleagues and not just the ones we work with most often.

Continuing professional development

Continuing professional development (CPD) is the ongoing process of identifying and addressing learning needs and undertaking ongoing personal and professional development. It is a practice that professionals should undertake throughout their career; taking a focused approach to personal development through reflection and action can help to ensure career success, keep skills up to date, support personal motivation levels and, in a fast-paced world of work, help to ensure ongoing employability.

All workers, including remote and hybrid workers, should take CPD seriously. Ultimately, each individual is primarily responsible for their own learning and development. Arguably, this is equally true in an office or co-located environment too. A positive approach to lifelong learning is a skill for today and for the future.

CPD includes a range of activities. From the traditional training course to informal learning, mentoring or coaching, professional networking or simply reading a book or listening to a podcast – CPD is about addressing needs through the most appropriate way for the individual and the learning need itself.

Working remotely can bring both opportunities and challenges when it comes to managing CPD. Digital tools and virtual work can make learning and development more accessible than it sometimes is in a face-to-face environment. For example, it is possible to access webinars or virtual conferences from anywhere in the world without having to travel. Virtual learning (any learning that takes place in an online environment as opposed to a traditional classroom environment, usually supported by technology) is ever more commonplace through online courses. Outside of formal training there are many informal learning opportunities provided by digital technology such as blogs, TED talks and podcasts.

Depending on their preferred style of learning, not everyone finds online learning easy; some might find it hard to concentrate or miss interactions with other learners. When working from home exclusively, without on-hand learning and development opportunities such as face-to-face training courses, it might also be easy to neglect the process of CPD. With remote work also comes reduced opportunities to learn by watching other more experienced colleagues.

Regardless of personal preference, managing one's own CPD is a career essential. The process of CPD generally has several stages:

- self-assessment or reflection (where am I now, what gaps might I have)

- planning for learning and development (what do I need to do and how can I do it, setting goals)

- taking action (undertaking an activity to support learning and development, taking a step towards a goal)

- review (how did that go, what have I learnt, what do I need to do now or next)

Setting goals is a key part of CPD. We are all probably familiar with the simple acronym SMART (specific, measurable, achievable, relevant and timed). Objectives will be effective when they address each of these individual elements; without them objectives may be difficult to understand or implement, be too vague or impossible to achieve. SMART can be a helpful approach as long as goals are also reviewed regularly – whatever goals we set also need to be prioritized and capable of changing when circumstances do.

Taking time out on a regular basis to think about and plan for continuing professional development is a good habit to build. What amounts to CPD will vary for each individual. Documenting in some format is recommended, as this helps to maintain a record and identify achievements.

A good CPD plan should:

- take into account feedback from others, such as managers or mentors
- detail activities to be completed, aligned to both current role and future career aspirations
- set review dates
- provide an evaluation of successes and achievements
- for the newly remote worker or early-career professional, include CPD activities for developing and implementing the skills for remote and hybrid work themselves discussed in this book

---

EXERCISE
Developing your long-term goals

Part of career management is having a long-term goal or vision for your career. Do you have one? If not, consider reflecting on some of these questions:

- What does career success mean to you? What would having career success look or feel like?
- What do you want to achieve?
- What matters to you most at work and in your career? What gives your work meaning?
- What aspects of your current role do you enjoy the most – and which do you wish you could stop?
- What comes easily or naturally to you?
- What does your ideal working life look like? Consider this in terms of job, money, success and work–life balance.

TOP TIPS
Managing your remote career

- Even when they allow remote or hybrid working, not every company will be truly welcoming and accepting of remote work and remote workers. Think carefully about working with companies (or managers) who aren't truly remote advocates or don't truly empower their remote workforce.

- Remote and hybrid work is here to stay – so review the skills for remote work discussed in Chapter 1, and make these a focus of your continuing professional development.

- Consider seeking out a mentor who can support you with your career in general, or with remote work success in particular. Do you know anyone who is an effective remote worker who would provide any tips or guidance?

- Identify if your organization provides any support or training on any aspect of successful remote or hybrid work.

- Take a purposeful approach to professional networking internally and externally, remote and in person.

- Demonstrate your value – don't be afraid to share your successes and achievements. Remember: it isn't bragging if it's true! Don't rely on other people to talk you up. Be responsible for this yourself.

- Make the most of the freedom remote work gives you to work when you are at your best and at your most productive.

- Invest in your own development. This is standard career advice. It is imperative for all professionals to keep their skills up to date. Working remotely can bring new opportunities to do this, from attending remote conferences to online networking groups.

- Regularly review your current learning and development needs and identify activities to ensure your continuing professional development.

Summary points

Career management includes the process of setting career goals and aims, planning for continuing professional development, undertaking learning and development and building a professional network:

- Many of the career management techniques that a remote worker needs to use to support career success will be familiar to those who already take a planned approach to managing their career and personal development.

- Planning for careers and development is critical for all professionals – remote, hybrid or co-located – to ensure professional success. In a remote environment, however, there is the need to overcome some of the potential challenges of remote work or to be simply more focused and intentional in that planning process.

- Early-career professionals in particular, or those new to remote working, should make a specific plan for managing their career while working remotely, including building critical remote work skills.

08
Leading and managing remotely

Effective management and leadership is key to the success of remote and hybrid teams. Providing appropriate support to remote workers is one particularly important aspect. Leading and managing a remote team (whether fully or partly remote/hybrid) does not require an entirely new skill set. It does, however, require adaptation of approach and awareness of how to approach some of the specific challenges that can arise from leading in this revised way.

Many of those areas that we have long considered as critical for effective people management, such as effective performance conversations and the setting of clear objectives, become even more important when working remotely. Unfortunately, in some organizations these important aspects of people management just do not happen – this is a problem at any time but becomes even more problematic in a remote environment.

In the same way as with undertaking remote and hybrid work, there are some notable differences between leading teams that have some time in an office and together, and leading teams that are 100 per cent remote. In the former, the manager has the opportunity for regular face time and bringing team members together, even if it is just for occasional meetings and events. They do, however, also have to manage the complexities that this can bring, both practically (managing the logistics of who is where and when) and ensuring fairness and inclusion. In a completely remote team every aspect of management has to be undertaken virtually and through the use of technology.

There are some aspects of leading and managing remote teams that are undoubtedly more difficult. Although the skill set for remote management is indeed similar to that for office-based management, some traditional advice around good management practice will no longer hold true. It is simply not possible to manage a remote team in the same way as a co-located, office-based team; to do so will be a route to failure and may result in poorer working relationships, reduced team effectiveness, or mistakes and miscommunications. Leading differently will require an element of letting go – letting go of personal working preferences, of the need to control or monitor, or simply of past beliefs about the 'right' way to lead and manage. There is simply no way that managers of a remote team can be aware of everything that their team is working on – instead, they have to empower employees to work autonomously. Many of the traditional ways that managers manage involve physical presence and contact – remote work reshapes these traditions and relationships.

One of the biggest challenges of leading a remote team is finding the right balance between being close to a team and available for them, while not micro-managing or being overbearing. It is easy to be either too hands-on, or too hands-off. Each team member may also require a different level of supervision and support. Research does tell us that people benefit from and welcome autonomy – it is also a key motivator. Key principles of remote work therefore should include autonomy – trusting that people will do their best, wherever or whenever they are working.

Managers and leaders of remote and hybrid teams also have responsibilities around well-being and supporting work–life balance, diversity and inclusion, and communication. They will need to know how to recruit remotely, and induct new remote starters. Leaders of remote teams also need to be competent users of technology, as much communication and collaboration takes place through it. These are new not management skills – but they will require greater intentionality. Organizational culture influences how successful remote and hybrid working is in practice – and leaders and managers are an integral part of that culture. Some organizational cultures are better prepared for and accepting of remote work than others.

Appendix 2 (1) provides further guidance for managers of remote and hybrid teams, and Appendix 2 (2) describes some of the pitfalls to avoid.

Key skills for managers leading remote and hybrid teams

- **Communication.** As we have already discussed in Chapter 4, communication is a key skill for remote work. As a leader or manager, it is perhaps even more critical. Managers need to set the tone for communication in the team and role-model effective communication and collaboration.

- **Clarity of expectation.** When employees are not clear about what is expected of them, in terms of both their performance and the way that they should be working when undertaking remote and hybrid work, there is a risk of misunderstandings, mistakes or breakdown in trust and relationships.

- **Performance management.** Managers of remote teams need to be able not only to set effective objectives and goals for remote workers and teams, but also to effectively measure performance objectively, and not by relying on presence and proximity.

- **Relationship building.** The role of the manager is to build professional, meaningful and effective relationships with team members (wherever and whenever they work), as well as to build the same between members of the team.

- **Technology.** Managers need to be able to use whatever technology is in use in their organization. They must be able to role-model its use, and help other employees in using it too.

Specific technologies will change over time, so matter less than overall attitudes to using technology and keeping skills up to date.

- **Well-being.** Managers provide support for employees in establishing boundaries, balancing their work and life, and managing the potential for well-being risks such as isolation or work/home conflict. Managers also need to be able to spot the signs that someone isn't okay – and know how to have an appropriate conversation in these circumstances.

- **Removing barriers.** Some organizations, unintentionally, will have barriers to effective remote or hybrid working. These may be cultural, technological or behavioural. It is the role of leaders and managers to identify and remove these barriers, helping their remote workers to be successful and effective.

- **Ensuring fairness and equity between remote and non-remote employees.** Depending on the organization and the roles within it, managers may well find themselves managing teams of workers undertaking different levels of remote work, from full-time remote workers to occasional ones – or even people who cannot work remotely at all. Managers will need to ensure equality of approach and avoid any perceptions of unfairness or bias towards some groups.

- **Coaching.** When employees aren't immediately visible, a coaching style of management can lead to significant benefits. Coaching helps people to find their own solutions to their challenges, helping them to become more self-sufficient – key to remote work.

However, perhaps above all the most important thing that a remote leader or manager needs to do is build an environment of trust – something that is key to the success of remote work.

Arguably all of these skills apply to good people management at any time and in any circumstances. They would apply just as equally to managing a co-located team – when the team is remote, however, these skills need to be applied in a modified way.

Leading remote and hybrid teams is a skill set of its own – but one that can certainly be learnt.

> **Reflect**
>
> Review the skills for managing and leading remote teams. To what extent do you believe you currently have these skills? Do you have any development areas, and if so, how can you address these?

Challenges of leading and managing remote and hybrid teams

There can be a few key challenges to overcome in relation to managing and leading remote teams. These include:

- Ensuring effective team relationships, collaboration and communication when people are not co-located. In particular, making sure that everyone has all the information that they need to do their job properly – wherever they are working.

- In hybrid teams in particular, scheduling and managing the logistics of employees attending work on different days.

- Being aware of managing personal biases about flexible and remote work.

- Ensuring fairness, equity and inclusion for all team members, wherever and whenever they work. This is especially important when teams are hybrid as managers will need to make sure there is no 'in group' and 'out group'.

- Undertaking remote performance management, including providing clear objectives and identifying appropriate measures for performance.

- Becoming personally comfortable with not being able to see what people are doing in real time.

None of these challenges are insurmountable. When it comes to remote and hybrid work, each manager and leader is a powerful role model. Individuals will look to those more senior than them to determine what is, and what is not, an acceptable way to work.

Creating the culture

In earlier discussions on motivation we considered the work of Daniel Pink (2010) whose studies in the area helped us to understand that many people are not motivated by monetary rewards, but by autonomy, mastery (the ability or urge to improve or enhance skills) and purpose (doing something that has meaning). There is much that we can apply here to remote work in general, as well as motivation specifically.

Autonomy is about being self-directed and independent, with freedom to choose, especially in relation to how work is done. It assumes good intent; that employees themselves want to do a great job and most of the time are capable of deciding how to achieve just that. It aligns too with other areas explored in this book including the ability to rethink time and maximize well-being through aligning work with personal rhythms and work–life balance.

Mastery is linked to the desire to do a job well and to continue to improve and develop – not necessarily because reward is involved but for its own sake. Learning is also linked to positive well-being as it can drive a sense of personal accomplishment. When leaders support the development of mastery and provide autonomy, together these elements work to create a remote culture in which individuals can do their best work without the need for oversight or control, because they want to and not because they are being supervised.

Finally, purpose is about the bigger picture and individuals being able to see their place in that. It includes having common goals and outcomes. These common goals can help to unite a team, providing a clear sense of direction. This, with the techniques discussed elsewhere in this chapter relating to creating common ways of working, will empower teams and individuals, providing meaning and focus.

Reflect

To what extent does your current management or leadership style embody these principles? To what extent does your team have true autonomy or a shared purpose? How are you supporting the development of mastery in team members? Consider where you can introduce these ideas and principles into your leadership and management practice.

To summarize, successful remote working culture is sustained through:

- demonstrating the critical skills of remote leadership
- building trust
- supporting autonomy and mastery
- providing purpose
- providing great role models

Tip

If you are leading a hybrid team, you need to be a hybrid worker yourself – or have at least experienced hybrid working. This will allow you to understand the hybrid experience, become fully conversant with hybrid working technologies and help to prevent bias towards co-located team members. If you come into the office every day, this will encourage your team to do the same. If for any reason you decide not to work hybrid, be sure to explain this is your personal choice and not an expectation of others.

Deciding who can work flexibly

The specific challenges (and therefore some of the skills required) relating to leading and managing remotely will to some extent depend on remote maturity; is the team already remote and made up of experienced remote workers? Alternatively, is this a change of approach for a team who were formally office-based, or are employees asking their manager to work remotely for the first time? In the latter case, an important first step might actually be assessing whether a role can even be undertaken remotely or in a hybrid way. Not all roles are suitable for remote (or hybrid) working. Sometimes this will be obvious because of the nature of the work itself, but there may be circumstances in which you are asked to consider a request for remote working from a member of your team and it is not immediately clear if remote work is viable.

The role itself should be the primary driver in determining whether a role can be undertaken remotely or from home, but the individual and their suitability for remote work is also relevant. Considering firstly the employee's job description and day-to-day activities:

- What percentage of the tasks need to take place at a certain location? What percentage could take place elsewhere?

- What is the nature of the work being undertaken? How much of the work requires synchronous or asynchronous collaboration? How much requires independent work or work that requires supervision? How much of the work is routine or standardized?

- Can the different types of tasks be organized in such a way that they can be undertaken together, on specific days?

- Does the individual have the necessary skills to work from home, or can these skills be developed?

- What might the impact be of remote work on colleagues or other stakeholders?

- What are the potential benefits and disadvantages of remote work, in this particular context?

Where the answers to these questions are not easily identifiable, consider undertaking a trial of remote or hybrid working over an agreed time period.

Establishing remote ways of working

The first step for effectively managing remote or hybrid workers is to set some clear ground rules about how the team will work together and what is expected of individuals. There are benefits to collectively co-creating expectations around ways of working; this will give a team a sense of ownership and accountability. Areas suitable for team discussion and agreement include:

- How often the team will meet and how those meetings will take place; for example, will some meetings take place in person or will they all be virtual?

- What channels of communication will be used for what specific purposes? This may include how communication will take place but also when – especially important if a remote team works across multiple time zones.

- How will work be coordinated? This may include specific tasks, but also (in a hybrid team) coordination of time in the office or with each other.

- What technologies should the team use to undertake individual and shared work? What shared online spaces may be required, and how should these be established and maintained?

- How will the team share when and where they are working (especially important in a hybrid team)? Are there any particular times that the team will aim to work synchronously for collaboration purposes?

- What are the most appropriate ways to update on work, activities and objectives?

EXERCISE
Setting ground rules

Engage your team in discussing and agreeing ground rules for remote or hybrid working. Get the team together (virtually or in person) to discuss the questions set out above. Invite everyone to contribute to determine a team charter or set of principles to ensure successful remote working. Share those principles or rules with the team and any new starters to ensure clarity on expectations.

Having local, documented rules can support new starters, and make it clear to all team members what is expected of them. The leaders of hybrid or remote teams should communicate these rules clearly to all team members.

Building your remote team

Employees are individuals, with their own unique perspectives, motivations, aims, personal circumstances and concerns. Getting to know people and building a personal relationship with them is always important, but becomes more so in a remote environment when day-to-day interaction might be reduced and scheduled connections replace informal engagement. (See Appendix 2 (3) for more guidance on recruiting and 2 (5) on supporting new remote and hybrid workers.)

For example, personal motivations vary. Some people are motivated by money and recognition, whereas others are motivated by other factors such as the opportunity to make a difference, develop themselves or achieve formal qualifications. Some employees will be very career orientated; others may be more focused on family and activities outside of work, and for whom work is a means to an end. There is no right or wrong here in terms of the employee – but where a manager understands these individual perspectives and personal situations they can adapt their approach to help them get the best from their teams.

This knowledge can be built through 121s, career conversations, team meetings and regular dialogue between the manager and individual team members. Simple techniques such as regularly asking how people are, enquiring (appropriately) about their life outside of work, and showing an interest in them as individuals rather than just focusing on operational priorities can go a long way to supporting effective working relationships. These techniques can be employed just as well in a virtual and remote environment as they can in the office.

When teams are remote or hybrid, they may interact less. Even when there are plenty of communication channels, some of the more casual and social interactions of work can be lost. Managers can play a key role in enabling team members to build strong relationships and create connections. There are many ways through which this can be achieved. First of all, take opportunities to create social interaction. This can include creating an online space just for chat and informal interaction, providing space within virtual meetings (such as at the beginning or end) where people can just chat, holding events such as quizzes or competitions, celebrating birthdays or special occasions and encouraging mentoring or buddying relationships.

Tip

If you are managing a hybrid team, try to ensure that there are regular (perhaps weekly or monthly) opportunities to coordinate time together as a team, where every team member will be in the office or co-located. This might mean designating a specific day or activity, which everyone can have in their diary as a regular event. It should be an expectation that everyone attends these events. Make sure that the team understands the purpose of this time: building and supporting relationships.

Not everyone enjoys working remotely, or is able to do so effectively. Leading a remote team therefore may involve discussions with individual team members about their ability to work successfully from home or other remote location. The Remote Work Readiness Assessment in Appendix 1 (1) can support managers with these discussions. Some employees may need support and guidance in becoming effective remote workers; others may find that it is unsuitable for them for a range of reasons. Where this is the case, managers may wish to explore alternatives, such as the opportunity to co-locate permanently with colleagues.

Reflect

How effectively are your remote team members working together currently? What are their strengths and weaknesses, and what improvements are required to ensure long-term success?

Communicating with your remote team

The subject of communication has already been explored in Chapter 4. Good communication is a key business and leadership skill at any time, but leaders of remote teams have a particular responsibility to be role models for great communication. There are slightly different communication challenges to overcome depending on whether a team is fully remote or hybrid (working from home just some of the time). Hybrid teams may, depending on their working arrangements, come together from time to time, thereby opening up new communication methods and opportunities.

Managers of remote teams should also review the guidance in Chapter 4 on holding effective virtual meetings.

When teams work remotely, communication needs to be much more explicit and intentional; this is partly the responsibility of the manager of the team. Team members also have a key role to play, but when managers lead from the front and focus on the importance of great communication this helps to send a signal about what is expected of others.

Tip

Everyone's experience of remote work is different. How you feel about remote work, or the benefits and challenges you experience, may be very different to your employees' perspectives. Don't assume you know how your team members feel. Take the time in 121s to check in often.

Managing the performance of your remote team

Effective performance management is critical in all situations, whether remote, hybrid or in a traditional co-located environment, and it is perhaps one of the most important skills for people managers to possess. The term refers to the combination of activities (and often processes and procedures too) that includes setting objectives, managing motivation, performance appraisal, supporting learning and development, reward and recognition. It also includes the management of underperformance. Performance takes place at a team level and at an individual one.

Performance management activities will typically take up a significant amount of managerial time. When undertaken well, they can contribute to the development, motivation, engagement and retention of employees.

Managers need to ensure that they have effective mechanisms for managing remote performance. One of the biggest adjustments is the way work is measured. Instead of observable actions, measurement of performance has to focus on outcomes and outputs, contribution and results. Above all, these mechanisms for managing performance must *not* be based on the hours that people work.

Here is where we see the importance of those basics of good performance management: setting clear objectives that are also realistic and time bound; confirming (where appropriate) key performance indicators or other clear measures so that each employee knows how they will be assessed; and the provision of regular feedback. It is all too easy in any working environment for objectives to get out of date, and performance conversations to be forgotten when day-to-day priorities take precedence. In remote teams it can be helpful for team members to have visibility, or at least an awareness, of the objectives or priorities of others; consider encouraging the team to share their objectives with each other where appropriate.

Work that takes place remotely is by its very nature less visible. It can be tempting therefore to think that it will be much harder to manage performance in a remote environment – but this isn't necessarily the case. When we are in a traditional office environment it is very rare that we have full visibility of the work of our team. However, we often conflate presence with performance. We believe that if we can see people they must be working. In fact, research suggests that when we see people working, especially when we see them working long hours, we tend to attribute certain traits to them. We believe them to be more committed and motivated – even if we have no evidence at all upon which to base this. It is a form of unconscious bias. Unfortunately, it also sometimes translates into who we reward, promote and recognize. The first step for managers therefore is to be aware of this potential and guard against it, especially when it comes to managing performance as well as providing opportunities for development, reward or recognition.

Before we can truly start to manage and assess performance, we must start with a critical question: *What do we mean by performance?* Academic literature considers that individual job performance should be defined as those things that people actually do as a part of their job. This includes the actions that they take which contribute to the organization's goals (Campbell and Wiernik, 2015). This might not be the same as the outputs from the things that they do. Individual performance should be assessed on what those individuals have within their control. If we accept this definition of performance, it follows that we cannot understand and assess performance without first having a clear scope of what the employee should do, has done or is doing, or how that individual contributes. The employee needs to truly understand this too. This sounds simple, but is not always true in practice.

We can break performance management down into several discrete phases: setting goals and objectives, effective conversations, and measuring and reviewing performance. These areas will now be explored in turn.

Setting goals and objectives

Without objectives it can be difficult to formally assess achievement or success. Objectives should support employees by providing clarity on what needs to be done, and enable the performance appraisal process by providing a standard against which the manager can assess the individual, but against which the individual can also assess themselves. Objectives, both team and individual, should also align with wider organizational strategy, goals and objectives. It is important for everyone to see the part they play in the bigger picture. Goals also help managers to hold people accountable for their work – and take ownership of it. Remote work is generally more autonomous as workers are more independent and do not have immediate supervision. Goals therefore become even more important than ever.

Many people will already be familiar with the acronym SMART, already discussed briefly in Chapter 7 on career management. This is a standard approach to the setting of objectives, and stands for specific, measurable, achievable, relevant and timed. The idea behind SMART is that an objective will be most effective when it addresses each of these individual aspects. Without these elements an objective may be difficult to understand or implement, or be too vague for employees to understand how they can be deemed successful. In a remote environment taking a SMART approach will not only provide clarity of requirements but also provide a way of assessing performance that does not rely on presence or being seen in the office.

SMART is a good starting point but it is not all that an employee needs. Today's world is fast changing and agility is critical – for both individuals and organizations. Objectives must therefore also be agile, as well as SMART. It will not always be possible to set goals and plans a year in advance and not review and update them over that time period. When circumstances change, so must goals and objectives.

Shared goals or a shared team vision can help to bring remote teams together, providing a common purpose regardless of location and specific job function. Every team should have a purpose and be clear how their work contributes to broader organization goals. Where appropriate, managers should also share their own personal objectives and goals with the team. However, when setting shared goals, ensure that each individual is aware of their own specific contribution to that goal. Otherwise there is the potential for what is sometimes known as 'social loafing' where one person puts in less effort, letting the rest of the group do the bulk of the work. Unchecked, this can lead to team conflict, a building sense of unfairness and hiding underperformance.

Objectives should therefore:

- be SMART
- be aligned to organizational strategy and plans
- be adaptable to changing circumstances
- be a mixture of team and individual
- provide some 'stretch' (challenge or development)

Reflect

Do all the members of your remote or hybrid team have clear, measurable objectives? Do they know exactly what is expected of them and how their performance will be assessed? Be sure to update objectives, and talk about them, on a regular basis.

Effective conversations

When managers and their teams are not co-located and work is less visible, there is a greater need for regular conversations about performance. The formal performance review is just one way to discuss performance in the workplace but it should not be the only one. Effective performance conversations can be informal – and ideally they will be continually taking place.

Talking about performance on a regular basis will help to ensure that objectives do not become stale and irrelevant, development needs are addressed quickly, and feedback can become a regular activity rather than an annual event to be feared. Regular conversations also help to create the conditions for a feedback of culture and open discussion.

Managers of remote teams need to build in deliberate time for 121 contact with every member of their team. When a manager is not constantly co-located with their team there are fewer opportunities for casual chats or check-ins. This could lead to employees feeling isolated, but could also mean that a struggling employee could go unnoticed for too long. Regular 121 meetings give employees the opportunity to raise concerns and issues, as well as providing a space for discussions about objectives, progress or development. These meetings are a vital part of building effective relationships between managers and their team members. How often these meetings should take place will vary depending on the role, individual and organization. A good practice approach would be for managers to meet with the people that work for them on at least a monthly basis in whatever format works for them both. Depending on the role and the individuals concerned, however, this may be too often or too infrequent – managers may therefore wish to talk to each team member about what is an appropriate frequency. A successful regular remote 121 should include:

- updates or a check-in on current projects and activities
- a review of progress against current objectives
- a well-being check
- a check-in around any support required or current challenges and problems
- feedback or recognition where appropriate
- just like in a face-to-face environment, when performance issues arise they must be tackled quickly to avoid them escalating.

Appendix 2 (4) provides further guidance on undertaking a successful virtual 121 with your team members.

Measuring and reviewing performance

How performance is measured will differ from organization to organization, and will be influenced by the type of work being undertaken or the industry or sector – as well as the individual. Monitoring and measurement can range from a senior employee simply observing work tasks through to automation of monitoring through sophisticated tracking systems.

The rise of remote working during the Covid-19 pandemic also gave rise to the development of remote monitoring tools, designed to assess the productivity of those who could not be physically supervised. While managers *can* use these tools, that does not mean that they *should*. On a practical level these tools can often be easily circumvented or the outcomes manipulated. From a cultural perspective they are not likely to generate a high trust environment, making employees feel micro-managed and disengaged. When employees have low autonomy and are subject to high degrees of control this can also lead to work-related stress. There are much better ways to measure and appraise the performance of remote workers such as setting effective objectives or using relevant key performance indicators.

Each role will require its own form of measurement specific to the work undertaken and the requirements of the job. This could include achievement against target, tasks completed, time taken to complete activities, customer satisfaction, accuracy or items produced. When it comes to setting measurements keep these three rules in mind:

1 The individual must understand what is being measured and how they can succeed.

2 What is being measured must be under the control of the individual.

3 Measurement should include what the individual did – and not merely the outcome of those activities.

Too often we place all our attention on the outcome of activities. However, this is not always appropriate as the outcome may be outside of the control of the employee, influenced by external factors such as pricing, the economy or the actions of others.

Reflect

How will you assess performance that you cannot physically see taking place? For each of the people who work for you, how will you assess their success? How can you make sure that they understand this?

When managers and their employees meet regularly there can be a temptation to spend a great deal of the time on operational matters or business updates. This is not necessarily a problem as long as some time is also set aside to discuss performance in general. In addition to the shorter, monthly catch-up meetings discussed earlier, managers may wish to consider some of the following, all of which can be undertaken virtually:

- At least once a quarter review (and update as necessary) any objectives from the last formal performance review where these are undertaken. Check progress against objectives.

- Check in with the employee after any learning or development activity to review it – and discuss any follow-up that is required.

- At least once a quarter revisit any learning or development plan to check if it is still current, and if any part of it needs to be updated or removed, or if anything new needs to be added.

- Make it a habit throughout the year to seek feedback on your team members from individuals who have useful insights or information. Do not wait for a formal performance review cycle – memories may have faded by then and people often get multiple requests at this time of the year. This will offset any lack of visibility of work that might result from the nature of remote work.

- Where employees have performed well, make sure to recognize them at the time rather than wait for the performance review or any organizational cycle of reward (such as awards or pay rises).

- Set up a system for taking notes that you can add to on an ongoing basis throughout the year so that you have plenty of information available for discussion at formal performance management meetings.

- Discuss performance and contribution at the end of a particular project or piece of work that the employee has undertaken.

It may feel like there is a lot to consider in the list above, especially for managers who have a busy workload of their own. However, when employees are developed, communicated with and supported in learning in the longer term this will have a positive impact on the manager's own workload as they will have a more competent and committed team.

As a manager of hybrid teams, you should consider which meetings to undertake virtually and which to undertake in person. A mix of the two over the year is a good option.

In many organizations the main measure of performance is a formal (often annual) performance review meeting or appraisal. Performance review meetings themselves can also be undertaken face to face or virtually; it isn't the location that matters but the quality of the conversation. When a team works in a hybrid way, one option is to ask the employee their preference for either an in-person or virtual meeting. Each organization will have its own approach to conducting performance reviews (or appraisals). However performance is assessed, managers should take the time to explain the process to employees and what is expected of them in terms of input and preparation. A good performance review will take some time to look backward at recent performance and achievements, and also forward, to consider new objectives, future plans and new development needs.

Tip

Remember that the assessment of performance is subjective. Performance is rarely static. Be aware of the potential for recency bias (focusing too much on recent performance and not performance over the whole assessment period).

Typical good performance review practice applies in a remote environment in the same way as a co-located one:

- Prepare for the review by reflecting on the individual's performance throughout the review period, and seek feedback from other relevant stakeholders.

- Focus on evidence; performance review feedback should be evidence-based rather than just the opinions of the manager. Use available data or metrics where available.

- Ask the individual to undertake their own preparation; encourage them to reflect what has gone well or less well during the review period, and think about future objectives and development needs.

- Set aside time for an effective conversation, making sure to reduce opportunities for distraction or interruption. If the meeting is being conducted virtually, silence other notifications so that you can focus your attention on the employee.

- Ensure balance in the conversation. Performance reviews should be a two-way conversation; it is important that the manager does not do all the talking. Managers should ask questions to gather the views of the employee.

Tip

When assessing the performance of hybrid workers be aware of the potential for proximity bias. This is the tendency to unconsciously favour people in our immediate vicinity or whom we see most often. Where there is a variety of hybrid working patterns within a team this could lead to higher performance ratings of those more regularly in the office.

When the employee being reviewed is a remote worker, consider some of the following and provide feedback accordingly:

- How well does the employee collaborate and communicate with other remote or hybrid colleagues?

- How competent is the employee at using remote working technology and tools?

- Reflect on the skills required to be a remote worker set out in Chapter 1: to what extent does the employee have these skills and where might they need to undertake additional development?

- How well does the employee manage their time and productivity?

- Does the employee need any specific development in relation to hybrid or remote work?

Tip

You don't need to wait for performance reviews to acknowledge and recognize great performance. Catch people doing good work and tell them what you appreciate and value about them and their work.

Assessing team performance

As already discussed, shared goals and objectives across a team can help to build a sense of shared ownership and collaboration, and help team relationships to be built and developed – all essential in a remote team. Of course, assessment team performance begins with a question: *What does a high-performing remote or hybrid team look like?*

Teams come in many shapes and sizes, but high-performing remote teams typically have some of the following characteristics:

- individually and collectively they deliver on their objectives
- they are committed to their shared goals and purpose
- they consistently work effectively together, collaborating, communicating and sharing knowledge
- they have clear roles and responsibilities, and everyone understands the part they play
- everyone in the team has a voice and takes part in decisions
- they are autonomous and capable of self-direction
- they have high levels of trust

When assessing performance, consider the role the employee plays in the team as well as their individual performance.

Supporting career development remotely

Part of the role of the manager is to support the development of their team members. Managers should engage in regular conversations about career and professional development. Many of the techniques for supporting career development are the same as they are in a traditional office-based or co-located environment. As with other managerial skills we have discussed, they simply need to be applied slightly differently in a remote or hybrid situation. Learning and development should be part of those performance management conversations; these shouldn't be limited to just whether someone has completed the objectives assigned to them but whether they have grown and developed as a professional – and how they might continue to do so.

Career conversations

Part of performance management is encouraging people to think about their long-term future – and helping them with a plan to achieve it. This is what a career conversation is; it is about moving the discussion on from the next performance review period (whether that is a few months or the year to come) into a longer time frame and one that encompasses broader personal or career goals. A career conversation therefore usually exceeds the typical time frame of the typical performance review (often one year). A good career conversation will consider:

- the employee's feelings about their career to date
- their ambitions for the future, often over a time period of several years
- how these ambitions might be achieved
- what both the employee and their manager can do in order to support the realization of those ambitions

Career conversations can send a clear signal to employees that their manager is interested in their future and will help the manager get to know the individuals who work for them – their unique motivations, interests and goals. Career conversations do not need to be undertaken regularly – annually would more than suffice. A separate meeting isn't required as it can be included in the annual performance review/appraisal or with any other conversation about learning and development.

Just like a performance management conversation, a career conversation has two parts. First of all it is a discussion about aims and objectives and broad goals. The second part of the conversation should be about the steps that the employee (with support from their manager) can take to make these goals a reality.

The following questions can help to start and then structure a successful career conversation:

- What are your long-term goals?
- What is your ultimate career goal?
- What role would you like to have in two years, or five?
- What does career success look like to you in the future?
- What is important to you in your next role?
- What are the steps you would need to take to support your goals?
- What development do you need that will help you to achieve your goals?
- How can I support you in achieving your career goals?

Sometimes employees do not know what they want to do in the future, or may not be clear what opportunities exist within the organization. Where this is the case, encourage the employee to undertake some research about what is available for them in terms of training, qualifications, coaching or development programmes.

Career conversations are a key part of performance management and shouldn't be forgotten because someone is working remotely. Long-term career progression is just as important to remote workers as it is to office-based ones.

Coaching

Coaching is based on the idea that individuals typically have the solutions to their own challenges, and the process of coaching can help them to find these solutions by encouraging reflection and thinking. When people find their own answers to challenges or come up with their own plans they are also more likely to take action and be successful than when simply following other people's ideas or advice. Through effective coaching techniques, managers can therefore help remote employees to manage their own performance as well as their careers.

Coaching involves the manager asking questions of their employee in a way that will help to encourage them to think and reflect. It requires the manager to step back from a role that they may feel more comfortable with or used to – such as providing information, guidance and advice. Many managers are used to telling employees what to do. By the very nature of their position they are expected to have more experience or knowledge, but this does not necessarily mean that they have the right answer for the employee and their particular challenge. Instead, coaching encourages managers to assume that the employee can work out the answer for themselves. It is especially useful when working with remote employees; no manager can be on hand for every small issue or question an individual has when they are not working in the same space or at the same time.

Coaching signals to employees that they are trusted, and that they have autonomy – key cultural requirements in a remote environment. It also reduces long-term reliance on managers, freeing them up to do other things as well as empowering employees to take ownership and responsibility for their own work. These are key remote work skills.

Effective coaching questions are open (which means that they start with *why*, *what*, *where*, *how* or *when*) and short. A question should be just that – and not advice in disguise. They do not lead or confuse. They are not complex or too long. Their aim is to get the individual to think and come up with ideas for themselves.

Examples of coaching questions include:

- What would you like to discuss?
- What do you think?
- What are your options?
- What have you tried so far?
- Who can help you with this?
- What would you like to do?
- What progress have you made?
- What do you think your priorities should be?
- What is going well?
- What isn't going well or could have gone better?
- What would you like to do more of?
- What could you do differently?
- What are you planning to do next?

Just like remote work itself, successful coaching does rely on a shift in mindset from a manager, especially one who is more used to providing advice or simply being present in a face-to-face environment. It may also mean some 'letting go', in that the employee may identify approaches to solutions that are different to the one the manager him- or herself would have preferred.

Coaching does also require one particular skill; it requires a manager to become comfortable with silence. In a coaching conversation silence can be a sign that someone is thinking and reflecting. Their brain is active! The coaching manager must resist the temptation to jump in and fill that silence with their own ideas and solutions. This may at first feel uncomfortable, but it can be key to the success of the technique.

In order to implement a coaching management style with remote workers, managers can begin with identifying one or two questions from the list above that feel comfortable and introduce these into any suitable performance management conversation. Then afterwards take a few moments to reflect on the success of the question itself. Consider experimenting with different questions and review their impact and effect.

EXERCISE
Developing performance management skills

Are your performance management skills ready for remote and hybrid workers? Reflect on these questions and answer simply yes or no:

- I schedule regular 121 meetings with all of my team to keep in touch and provide regular feedback.
- I don't wait for the formal performance review meeting to talk about performance with my team.
- All of my team currently have up-to-date and relevant objectives which are kept under review and updated throughout the year.
- All of my team understand how their performance will be assessed and measured.
- I check my own assessments of performance for potential bias.
- I prepare fully for all my formal performance review meetings and ensure that my team do the same.

- I always address poor or underperformance promptly with the individual employee.

- I adopt a coaching approach to empower my team.

- I review performance against set and communicated metrics and use evidence in my discussion.

- I provide feedback that is balanced, and is constructive rather than critical.

- Throughout the year I make notes about the performance of my team, so that when it is time for the formal review meeting I have a range of information and data to inform my feedback and performance rankings.

- The formal objectives that I set for my team are challenging and help them to develop without being too stressful.

As a result of these reflections, where do you need to make any changes?

TOP TIPS
Leading remotely

1 Take an individual approach. Talk to your team about what they need from you and the best way for you to communicate when working remotely.

2 Be a good role model for effective work-from-home practice. If you don't work flexibly then your team may not feel that they can do so either. Share how *you* work.

3 Be clear with your team when and how they can contact you when you are working remotely. Consider setting aside some time each week where you will be available for informal conversation or simply open up an online space that anyone can drop into.

4 Focus on communication. Communication in remote teams is a shared responsibility, but as the manager or leader of the team this will be driven by you. Also, be a good role model for communication.

5 Ensure that your team have clear and up-to-date objectives so that they fully understand how their performance will be assessed and measured.

6 Be aware of your own potential for bias. When allocating work or considering who to reward and recognize, are these decisions based upon performance and contribution or are they based upon the person you see most regularly?

7 Challenge 'presenteeism' when you see it. Presenteeism has the potential to spread quickly, if people come to believe it is the way to get noticed or recognized. If you see someone regularly working long hours or outside of their normal working hours, initiate a conversation with them.

8 Address any performance concerns promptly. There is no reason to think that anyone working remotely will be any less productive or perform less well. However, if performance issues do arise they will rarely get better on their own account.

9 On an ongoing basis, support remote workers (both new and existing team members) to understand the organization's goals, vision and objectives, helping to ensure they don't become cut off from broader awareness of the business and their role within it.

10 Check in on well-being regularly – the signs and symptoms that someone is not okay are harder to spot when working remotely. If you want to know how people are, you will need to ask them often.

11 Pay special attention to new starters to your team and make sure to help them build relationships with their team and understand organization culture at a distance.

12 Encourage and participate in social events taking place virtually, or in person from time to time. This will help to build and maintain bonds between teams.

13 Work on both showing trust to your team and encouraging an environment in which colleagues trust one another. Trust is a fundamental part of successful remote work. It can take a while for trust to build in a remote team, so consider actions and activities that will promote trust.

Summary points

- Managers cannot rely on the old ways that they used to get things done in an office. This is unlikely to lead to long-term success.

- Leading and managing remote and hybrid teams requires significantly more focus on performance management, communication, objective setting, and team collaboration and cohesion than in a co-located environment.

- Leading and managing remote and hybrid teams does not necessarily require an entirely new skill set – but managers and leaders must adapt their approach if they are to be successful. You cannot manage a remote (or hybrid) team in the same way you manage a co-located team.

- Managers and leaders need to focus on building trust. It is a key foundation of remote work. Micro-management or old-style 'command and control' management is not an option.

- Enabling autonomy, mastery and purpose can all support successful remote work at a team and individual level.

- The manager and leader can be a powerful role model in creating healthy remote and hybrid working cultures.

09
Final thoughts

Remote working is now a key part of working life in many organizations, industries and sectors. The move to remote working was accelerated significantly by the Covid-19 global pandemic, meaning that both employees and the organizations that they work for had to learn to adapt at speed. Roles that would perhaps have previously been thought unsuitable for remote working were nonetheless transferred to the home during 2020. Hybrid work is the evolution of the enforced working-from-home period, and presents a new range of challenges.

Remote work is more than simply 'where work takes place'. It forces us to fundamentally rethink some of the ways we have worked and some of our beliefs about work. It challenges our ideas about the link between presence and performance, the office as default, the timing of work, and how we collaborate and communicate.

Hybrid and remote are similar but subtly different, and they therefore require different approaches depending on the specific situation. This includes differences in both undertaking the work and in leading and managing it.

Working remotely demands new and revised skills if individuals are to be confident of career success. Remote working allows us to think differently about work. We no longer need to be shackled to the 9 to 5, eight-hour day or five-day week based in an office. We can truly work anywhere, or any when. Although the institution of the office is unlikely to disappear in the short term – and in fact, few people want it to – remote work and hybrid work is clearly here to stay.

When embracing remote work, as individuals or organizations, it is not about simply replicating former office approaches in a new location (often our home) but taking opportunities to completely redesign and rethink work. The first step in this journey to better work is for individuals to be personally successful at undertaking remote work, and where applicable, successful at supporting others who work for them to do the same.

As remote and hybrid work becomes more embedded and more common, perhaps we will in the future stop referring to it as remote work at all. It will simply be called 'work'.

Summary points

- There is no such thing as best practice when it comes to remote and hybrid working – only what is the best fit for the particular role, organization and circumstances. What makes remote or hybrid work successful in one organization will not necessarily transfer to another. Context is everything and employees need to be able to adapt.

- Remote and hybrid ways of working require the development of new skills in order to ensure career success, as well as other more familiar skills to be applied in new ways.

- Remote and hybrid work does not suit every role – or indeed every individual. Some people will thrive working remotely whereas others will be more successful and happy in an office environment. Self-awareness is part of the journey towards success.

- The skills for remote and hybrid work are similar – but not entirely the same.

- The skills for remote and hybrid working can be learnt. This is the responsibility of the remote worker, with support from their manager and internal learning and development teams.

- Remote and hybrid work demands high-level skills in communication, self-organization, digital capabilities and personal well-being management.

- Leading and managing remote teams demands similar skills to those relevant to in-person or co-located leadership – but some aspects of leadership and management become more important or need more intentional focus.

- Remote work is at its most transformational when combined with other forms of flexible working, particularly time flexibility and asynchronous work. Here we will see the fullest benefits to both individuals and their organizations.

- Remote and hybrid working is highly desired by employees – and this demand is only likely to increase in the future, especially as we continue to learn how to fully optimize its potential and new technologies continue to develop.

- Remote and hybrid work will continue to evolve and change over time; it is firmly a part of the future of work.

Appendix 1

Resources for remote and hybrid workers

This Appendix provides some resources designed to support you if you are currently a remote worker – or hope to be!

1. Remote work readiness assessment

Try this remote work readiness assessment to establish whether you are ready to effectively work remotely as well as identify where you need to make changes. These questions can also help potential hybrid workers. Ask yourself the following questions:

- Do you have a suitable space at home in which you can work effectively and privately?

- Do you have (or can you easily obtain) an appropriate desk and chair, and other essential equipment to ensure a comfortable and safe workstation?

- Do you have a strong wifi connection that will support video calling and online collaboration?

- Can you meet all requirements and responsibilities of remote work set out in any of your organization's policies and procedures?

- Do you have (where relevant) appropriate arrangements in place for childcare or other caring responsibilities to ensure you can work safely and without interruption?

- Do you have awareness of the well-being implications of remote working, and do you have appropriate strategies in place to address these?

- Are you capable of maintaining an effective work–life balance, including managing the temptation to overwork?
- Review the discussion of skills for home working discussed in Chapter 1. Do you believe you have these skills in sufficiency to work from home effectively?
- Are you an excellent communicator? Can you use a range of different tools and mediums to support effective communication?
- Do you consider yourself capable of self-motivation and able to work without supervision?
- Are you able to avoid distractions that might arise in your home environment?
- Are you competent with a range of technologies and tools that enable working from home?
- Can you comfortably work alone, without regular in-person contact with colleagues or team members?
- Are you confident that you can develop your career and learn effectively while working remotely?
- Have you previously and successfully worked from home?

If you have said 'yes' to the majority of these questions, you may be suitable to undertake remote working. If you answered 'no' to five questions or more, reflect on how you can address these respective areas before applying for or undertaking remote work.

2. Making a remote (including hybrid) working request

Some countries have specific legislation about making a request to work flexibly, which will generally include remote or home work. Many organizations also have their own policies detailing how requests should be made and will be considered. Some organizations will empower managers and employees to agree this locally whereas others will have formal application processes to complete.

Any request for remote (or hybrid working) should follow relevant legislation and internal policies. Where such organizational policies exist they typically include responsibilities for the remote worker, such as health and safety or information security requirements. Prior to making an application, ensure that all such requirements can be met and be sure to confirm this on the application.

If you want to ask to work from home, the following tips may help you to formulate your request. Prior to making your application:

- Check if any other employees currently work from home. Is there a precedent for working remotely in your organization?

- Consider the potential benefits to the organization or your manager of you undertaking remote work. How will supporting you to work remotely benefit them?

- What are the potential challenges or disadvantages that may arise from allowing you to work remotely? How do you propose to overcome these?

- What costs may the organization incur if you are permitted to work in a remote way? How can these be mitigated, or how will the business benefit overall even if these costs are incurred?

- How do you propose to communicate and collaborate effectively with your team while working remotely?

- If you want to work in a hybrid way, set out how you plan to manage your time and detail your proposed working pattern, including what days you would be in the office.

- Detail each of these points in any application, along with detail of the proposal itself, including whether you propose to work remotely some or all of the time.

Also consider:

- Suggesting how the success of remote working can be monitored or measured, and over what time period this success can be evaluated.

- Try to pre-empt what concerns your manager may have about remote work. How can you reassure them?

- Where the potential of remote working cannot be immediately or easily assessed (perhaps, for example, because no other team members currently work in a remote way) propose a trial period during which overall success of remote working can be reviewed. A trial period could last for anything from a few weeks to several months.

- If you have worked remotely in the past, even at another organization, provide some information about how you approached it and created success.

3. 10 remote and home working pitfalls to avoid

When working remotely, especially for the first time, there are some common mistakes that individuals make. Avoid these 10 common remote working pitfalls if you want to ensure success:

1 **Overworking.** It is very easy when working from home for the working day to extend, either by starting early or finishing late, or failing to take a break. This can make us sedentary too, which is bad for general well-being. Working too many hours will make you unproductive and risk burnout. Set a regular finish time, take breaks throughout the day and try to get outside for fresh air.

2 **Never switching off.** An extension of the problem in point 1, when you work from home and have all of your work equipment to hand, it can be tempting to keep checking your emails or notifications. This can create fatigue and reduce rest and recovery time in between work tasks. Set clear boundaries including non-working time and manage notifications on your devices.

3 **Failing to manage interruptions**. All workplaces are full of disruptions, especially offices. Home workers have different potential interruptions. They may be sharing their workspace with other family members, or may become mentally distracted by home responsibilities. All home workers need an approach for managing interruptions that works for them.

4 **Not setting up a proper workspace**. It's fine if you only work from home occasionally to work from a temporary space like the kitchen table. This is not sustainable if you work remotely on a regular basis. Over time this may lead to musculoskeletal issues. Ensure you have a proper workstation that supports long-term use.

5 **Over-reliance on written communication**. Using predominantly email or messaging when working remotely is another habit that is easy to slip into, especially when we consider that remote working often also results in a proliferation of online meetings. An email often seems like a way of avoiding just more screen time. However, this can reduce opportunities to build relationships with and get to know colleagues. A mix of communication methods is generally preferable.

6 **Trying to manage other responsibilities while working**. Other than in a short-term emergency situation, remote workers should not attempt to simultaneously undertake work at the same time as family or caring responsibilities. This is not practical, may impact upon your ability to work effectively and professionally, and is often against work policies. Always have caring arrangements in place when working from home.

7 **Becoming isolated**. Isolation can be a feature of remote work. This may be a particular problem for those who live alone, work in different time zones to colleagues or who are generally more extroverted. It is important to still build in intentional time for social connection.

8 **Multitasking**. When working remotely many people find themselves multitasking. For example, joining an online meeting

while also responding to emails. Unfortunately, multitasking is a myth. We are actually switching between tasks and neither has our full attention. This can lead to poor quality work – not to mention embarrassing incidents when we are called upon in a meeting and weren't listening! Try to focus on one task at a time. Your brain will thank you for it.

9 **Being too available.** When working remotely we sometimes feel that we have to prove our productivity or availability – just in case someone might think we are taking advantage. This can lead to some of the issues in points 1 and 2. Don't fear not being immediately available – no one needs to be available 24/7.

10 **Still working 9 to 5.** When you work remotely, unless required to do so by your organization, there is no need to entirely replicate your office schedule. Tailoring working hours to personal working styles and rhythms supports well-being and productivity.

4. 10 tips for being an effective hybrid worker

Hybrid work is a very particular (and fairly new) form of remote work. Usually hybrid workers spend some time in the office and some time working from home. Although many of the tips for effective remote work apply to hybrid workers too, there are some additional areas to consider in order for you to create success:

1 **Plan your working week.** This will ensure you are aligning the work you are doing with the most appropriate environment in which to do it, and will help to optimize effectiveness. Take some time at the beginning of each week (or the end of the previous one) for planning. Don't try to put too much into the plan – keep some time for emergencies or urgent work.

2 **Flex your routine**. Remote days and office days will, and should be, different. Don't try to replicate your office days in your home office. There is no need to do so, and you might miss some of the many benefits of remote work if you do.

3 **Don't neglect your ergonomics**. Just because you are only working from home for some of the time, don't be tempted to work from a kitchen table or sofa – it is still important to set up a proper workstation.

4 **Focus on face time**. As hybrid work provides opportunities to work in a physical location with colleagues, make the most of this time. Don't go into the office to sit at your desk and send emails or do other virtual work that you can do in your remote working time. Arrange meetings with people, get face time with your manager or plan activities that are enhanced by in-person collaboration.

5 **Be visible when in the office**. Take the opportunity to be seen, especially by managers or key stakeholders. Consider where you locate yourself to enhance your visibility and support this with maximizing face time.

6 **Be inclusive**. When you are working in the office be sure to include remote colleagues in communications – especially meetings. Specifically invite colleagues to contribute even if they are not in the room. Be mindful of the potential for proximity bias – defaulting to the people in closest proximity. This will role-model good practice and help to ensure colleagues treat you in the same inclusive way when you are not in the office.

7 **Stay connected on remote days**. Although it makes sense to focus on independent tasks when not in the office, make the effort to still stay connected to colleagues on those days. This will help keep you visible – reducing isolation and supporting relationships.

8 **Communicate clearly where you are working and when**. Make sure that your colleagues, managers or customers know when

you will be in the office and when you will be working remotely, as well as your working hours. Use email auto-signatures and shared calendars. Let people know the best times to reach you.

9   **Manage boundaries.** Boundaries can be easier to maintain in office-based time but more challenging when working from home. Although you can't 'cut and paste' your office routine into your remote days (nor should you try), be mindful of recreating some of those boundaries to support organization and well-being. Use the guidance and tips in Chapter 5 of this book on well-being to help you.

10 **Do something with your (not) commuting time.** Not having to commute is one of the biggest benefits of remote or hybrid work. On the days that you are not commuting, deliberately use that time for something that improves your life or supports your well-being. Don't waste it!

When working in a hybrid way it is also a good idea to give some thought to what are the best days, for you, your role and your team, for you to be in the office and at home. Where possible, be flexible with these days to meet business needs. For example, it might be convenient to work from home on a Friday – it is the preference of many people – but is that the best day operationally or professionally? Consider the benefits of a fixed schedule versus a flexible one. Avoid treating all your working days the same – the benefits from hybrid will come from aligning your activities to the best place to undertake them.

5. Identifying your personal productivity

Working remotely can allow us to enhance our personal productivity by tailoring our activities to our working style, personal preferences or energies. Not everyone, however, is used to thinking about personal productivity, often because when we work in traditional offices we tend to follow the standard eight-hour working day, categorized by a sustained period of work followed by a break of around an hour, and another sustained period of work. This working pattern can be traced back to a time when many of us worked in factories and we all had to work in the same place at the same time. This is no longer true for many roles today. Identifying personal productivity can be particularly important for hybrid workers – this can support them in tailoring their work activities to the best time and place to undertake them.

Use the following questions to aid your reflections on your personal productivity:

- What does productivity mean to you? How do you know if you have had a productive day? What would have happened?
- What time of the day do you feel most energized or alert?
- What time of the day do you feel most creative?
- What days of the week do you feel most energized?
- When do you feel tired or lacking in energy? What makes you feel tired or lacking in energy?
- What type of work makes you feel engaged and energetic?
- *When* do you do your best work?
- *Where* do you do your best work?
- What are your most challenging tasks, and when do you find it best to tackle them?
- Who are you with when you do your best work?
- Where do you have you best ideas – and when?
- How often do you need to take a break? How long does a break need to be for you to feel rested?
- How long can you work before you lose your focus?
- What influences your personal productivity, positively or negatively? How does your productivity change over the day, week, or even the time of year?

Use these reflections to consider what are your most productive, creative or 'peak' hours. What opportunities do you have to align your working hours and practices with your personal productivity?

If you have found it difficult to answer any of these reflective questions, consider keeping a reflective journal for a day or two. Note down when you stop and start tasks and your perception of your energy and focus levels. Look out for any patterns that might emerge. You can also consider experimenting with early starts or late finishes, as well as different break times and lengths to see what works for you.

Appendix 2

Resources for remote and hybrid leaders and managers

These resources have been provided as quick reference tools for people managers, addressing some of the common challenges and topics that arise when managing a remote or hybrid team.

1. Tips for managers of hybrid workers

Although managing remote and hybrid teams have many similarities, there are a few areas where a different approach is required for a team that is spending just some of their time working remotely and some of it in an office. Consider some of the following tips and hints:

- You may need to be responsible for determining how much time employees can spend at home and how much time they need to spend in the office. Depending on the role this might involve rotas or schedules.

- Talk to people about their personal working preferences and the blend of hybrid that works for them. Some people may prefer more office time than others and vice versa. While you may not always be able to accommodate every preference, do consider what is possible operationally.

- Encourage the whole team to come together, even occasionally, for some co-located time. This might be one day a week or a quarterly away-day – whatever fits the circumstances.

- Think carefully about inclusion and fairness in the team. Make sure that you are not defaulting to those who are in the office more often, disadvantaging your more remote employees. How can you ensure that there is equal voice and opportunity within your team – wherever and whenever people are working?

- Talk to your team about tech. Are they equally able to be effective whether they are working remotely or from the office? Do they have access to everything they need wherever they are? Do they need any training?

- Manage meetings well. Review the guidance for hybrid meetings in Chapter 4 and be aware of the disadvantages that can arise – and take steps to ensure equality in meetings.

- Help people to understand where people are working and when – and be clear on your own availability and working arrangements, including when you are contactable for help and support.

- Ensure that you are aware of how to properly facilitate a hybrid meeting in a way that ensures equality and inclusion for all. Seek training if it is available from your organization.

2. 10 pitfalls to avoid when managing a remote or hybrid team

When leading or managing a remote or hybrid team, whether or not you work remotely yourself, there are some common mistakes that managers make. Avoid these 10 common remote working pitfalls if you want to ensure success for yourself and your team:

1 **Micro-management.** There are few circumstances in which excess supervision is a good idea. It creates a sense of distrust and can be a stressful experience for the person being managed. In a remote environment it is almost impossible to micro-manage people although some managers try to do so by using remote tracking software. Instead managers and leaders should focus on trust and providing autonomy.

2 **Not holding 121 meetings.** When teams work remotely incidental and casual conversation is reduced – there is no opportunity to chat in the office or corridor. So deliberate time needs to be carved out for checking in, catching up and feeding back. Scheduled 121s provide employees with certainty that they will get time with their manager on a regular basis.

3 **Having too many meetings.** When teams move to remote work they often replicate how they worked in an office – and that typically involves a lot of meetings. As we have explored in this book, too much screen time is bad for us, and a day full of meetings leaves us with little time to reflect and think. When working remotely, teams should make use of a variety of communication methods and asynchronous tools to communicate, rather than relying too much on meetings. Remember: if you only communicate via meetings, so might your team!

4 **Not setting common ground rules.** In a remote team everyone needs to know what is expected of them in terms of behaviour and ways of working. This helps individuals to meet expectations, supports clarity (especially important for new starters) and keeps everyone on the same page. Engage your team on what these local rules should be.

5 **Failing to talk about well-being.** The potential for a range of well-being-related issues in remote work, as discussed in Chapter 5, is high. For remote working to support well-being rather than detract from it, employees need to create strategies and boundaries. Not everyone will find this easy to do, and it is easy to get into poor habits. Managers therefore need to make well-being part of their ongoing dialogue with their team.

6 **Bias towards co-located employees.** Unfortunately we know that we can have unconscious bias towards people in closest proximity to us. It may just be easier to communicate with people we see more often, and easy to forget to update those that are remote. Managers must be aware of this potential for bias and guard against it, ensuring that they treat everyone fairly, especially when communicating and providing opportunities for recognition and development. Otherwise a sense of unfairness will develop across the team.

7 **Neglecting relationship building.** Truly effective professional relationships will not arise by default. Managers need to dedicate time to building relationships both with their team, as well as facilitating them across their team too. In a remote environment this will require focused attention and time.

8 **Out of hours contact.** In a truly flexible organization that also embraces time flexibility and autonomy, arguably there is no need for formal 'office hours' and people can be empowered to work when it is best for them. However, when managers send emails or are visibly working on weekends and late into the evenings, this behaviour can quickly spread. It can send a signal to employees that this is expected or desirable behaviour. If you do work outside of more typical working hours be sure to tell your team that this is because this is best for you and they do not need to respond until their own working schedule. Show respect for people's boundaries, and the rest of the team will follow.

9 **Not communicating enough.** While there is such a thing as too much communication, in a remote working environment managers need to communicate clearly and consistently to ensure that all team members have the information that they need in order to work effectively. Talk to your team about communication norms. Manager communication needs a mix of predictable, scheduled communication methods and creating space for informal and ad hoc communication too.

10 **Not role-modelling the behaviour you want to see.** When managing remotely or in a hybrid team, managers need to demonstrate clearly the behaviours that they want to encourage for their team. For example, when managers demonstrate clear boundaries, take breaks or use preferred technologies, their team will follow. Equally, when managers demonstrate poor behaviours such as digital presenteeism their team will similarly adopt these behaviours.

3. Recruiting remote and hybrid workers

When recruiting remote or hybrid workers, it is important to ensure that the job applicant has the relevant skills to work effectively. Previous experience of remote working is not necessarily essential; the skills for remote work can be learnt and developed.

Some of these tips can help to recruit successfully:

- When advertising opportunities, be clear about the degree of remote or hybrid working that is available and what travel or attendance to a central office location or face-to-face meetings is required.

- Review the skills set out in Chapter 1 for remote and hybrid work. Consider which ones are most relevant to the job you are recruiting for and plan interview questions that will identify if the candidate holds these skills.

- Review some of the specific interview questions for hybrid and remote workers set out in Chapter 7. Build some of these into the recruitment process, focusing on whether the role is hybrid or fully remote.

- Prior to any virtual interview make sure to confirm the technology that will be used – where possible use common platforms like Zoom or MS Teams with which candidates will already be familiar. If using bespoke or less common systems provide some guidance to the candidate on how to use them.

- Talk to candidates about their experience, if applicable, of working from home during the Covid-19 global pandemic. What did they learn about themselves during this time?

- Hold your interview in the place the successful applicant will spend most of their time in order to see them in that environment. If the role is 100 per cent remote, don't make someone come into an office for an interview – hold it online. For hybrid workers, aim to include a little of both in the process (if you have more than one stage) or focus on the place they will spend most of their time. If the hybrid role involves predominantly office work with a little remote, interview in the office, and vice versa.

- Share with the applicant how hybrid or remote work takes place in your specific organization or team, and provide the opportunity to ask questions about it.

- If the individual has never worked remotely in the past, talk to them about their expectations of remote work and why they think it would be suitable for them and the role that they have applied for.

- Take the time to ask the candidate what, should they be appointed, they would need from you or the organization to help them be a successful remote or hybrid worker.

4. How to undertake a successful virtual 121

A 121 meeting is typically a fairly informal meeting taking place outside of the formal performance review process. It is an effective part of performance management, ensuring regular dialogue between employee and manager. Virtual 121s with a remote worker are not necessarily that different from those that would be undertaken in person.

There is no set rule about how often they should take place, how long they should last or what technology should be used for the meeting itself. As with most aspects of performance management, managers may need to tailor this to the employee and their individual needs. New starters may require more regular 121s than established employees, and high performers may need fewer. It is good practice to have a 121 on a monthly basis. Managers can also ask the employee how often they would like to meet and if they have a preference for an online meeting or even a phone call.

A 121 meeting is an opportunity to catch up on operational matters, check in on progress against objectives, talk about support and learning requirements and discuss priorities. Regular 121s can help to build relationships between employee and manager and ensure effective communication. It is tempting in an online meeting to jump straight into the agenda. From a relationship point of view do take the time to check in with the individual first. It is an opportunity to explore any particular aspects of remote work that can be challenging. Consider asking the individual some of the following from time to time:

- Do they feel that they have all of the information that they need to do their job effectively?
- Do they have the necessary tools to work remotely?
- What do they enjoy about working from home? Is it working effectively for them?
- How are they managing their well-being and work–life balance?
- What support do they need to be a more effective remote worker?

5. Supporting new starters to work remotely

Some new team members may be well versed in remote work already. For others this might be their first time working in a remote or hybrid team, requiring more focus and support. Regardless of whether someone is an experienced remote worker, however, they will need support to get up to speed. Joining an organization is very much a social process; it includes interactions with others, informal learning and making connections. The speed at which people develop relationships with other employees is an important factor in the overall success of an induction process.

The following tips can help create the conditions for a new starter in a remote team:

- Don't let the employee spend too much time working on their own in the early days – they may feel isolated and that lack of connection can feed into decisions to stay or leave.

- Make sure that the new team member has all of the equipment that they need to do their job effectively from Day One, wherever or whenever they are working. This should include access to all relevant systems, shared areas or online team groups or communication channels.

- If the team has any informal or local rules about working remotely, make sure that these are shared with the new starter. These might include agreements about shared calendars, updating and checking in, or meeting protocols. In a hybrid team this might also include how often team members attend the office in person.

- Help them understand the organization's culture. Every organization has its own culture and ways of working, but these can be harder to assimilate at a distance. In the induction period, make sure to share relevant information on the organization's values, mission and vision, as well as strategic aims and objectives.

- Have a dedicated team 'meet and greet' virtual meeting so that everyone can introduce themselves and their jobs, briefly, to the new starter and say an initial informal hello which can then be followed up with more detailed meetings where required.

- Encourage other people in the team to be proactive in building relationships with new team members – don't leave it up to the new starter but ask everyone to play their part in the welcome process.

- Facilitate meetings between the new team member and their wider team, as well as any key contacts or stakeholders. Meetings can be virtual or face to face if the team is hybrid. Provide a mentor or buddy too. This will help to support the individual during their first few critical weeks, as well as help them to feel part of the team and build relationships.

- Build in some social connection during the first few weeks. This could be an informal coffee or lunch (virtual or face to face), an invitation to any social groups or (in a hybrid team) a tour around the office and local area.

- If a new starter is going to work in a hybrid way, for their first few weeks ask them to be on site more often than they might normally be when they are established – this will help to speed up the process of getting to know the organization and understand culture. Make sure that there are colleagues in the office and available to support them.

- If the new starter is an inexperienced home worker, provide them with a buddy or a mentor who has much more experience with remote or hybrid work and can help them to navigate any early challenges.

The following questions can help you to discuss remote working with new remote or hybrid team members:

- What do you want to know or learn more about?

- What will help you to feel connected to our organizational culture or our team?

- How can I support you during your induction period?

- Do you have the information and tools you need to work effectively?

- Are you clear on what you need to do and what is expected of you?

Also review the resources on effective 121 meetings when working remotely to make the most of your meeting time with any new starter. During the induction period consider whether it is appropriate to hold these more frequently than you may usually hold them with your established team.

REFERENCES AND FURTHER READING

The following books, articles and academic research have helped to shape the content of this book and may be useful additional reading and resources for those who wish to learn more about remote work.

Research into working from home during Covid-19

Bailenson, J N (2021) Nonverbal overload: A theoretical argument for the causes of zoom fatigue, *Technology, Mind and Behaviour*, 2(1), doi.org/10.1037/tmb0000030 (archived at https://perma.cc/7VWX-WNNX)

Barrero, J M, Bloom, N and Davis, S J (2021) Why working from home will stick, Working Paper 28731, National Bureau of Economic Research, www.nber.org/papers/w28731 (archived at https://perma.cc/6CZE-H2BA)

Chung, H, Hyojin, S, Forbes, S and Birkett, H (2021) Working from home during the Covid-19 lockdown: Changing preferences and the future of work, University of Birmingham/University of Kent, www.birmingham.ac.uk/Documents/college-social-sciences/business/research/wirc/epp-working-from-home-COVID-19-lockdown.pdf (archived at https://perma.cc/DRX7-9D67)

CIPD (2019) Flexible working in the UK, Chartered Institute of Personnel and Development, www.cipd.co.uk/Images/flexible-working_tcm18-58746.pdf (archived at https://perma.cc/6GCG-GQDU)

Longqi,Y, Holtz, D, Jaffe, S, Siddharth, S, Shilpi, S, Weston, J, Joyce, C, Shah, N, Sherman, K, Hecht, B and Teevan, J (2021) The effects of remote work on collaboration among information workers, *Nature Human Behaviour*, www.nature.com/articles/s41562-021-01196-4 (archived at https://perma.cc/95Q8-NPZ4)

Remote and flexible work (and its consequences)

Baker, M (2021) 4 modes of collaboration are key to success in hybrid work, Gartner, www.gartner.com/smarterwithgartner/4-modes-of-collaboration-are-key-to-success-in-hybrid-work/ (archived at https://perma.cc/PN7A-JZWE)

Campbell, J P and Wiernik, B M (2015) The modeling and assessment of work performance, *Annual Review of Organizational Psychology and Organizational Behavior*, 2, 47–74, doi.org/10.1146/annurev-orgpsych-032414-111427 (archived at https://perma.cc/NJN4-7EFK)

Cristea, I and Leonardi, P (2019) Get noticed and die trying: Signals, sacrifice and the production of facetime in distributed work, *Organization Science*, 30(3), 552–72, doi.org/10.1287/orsc.2018.1265 (archived at https://perma.cc/4KEY-MQHF)

Dale, G (2020) *Flexible Working*, Kogan Page, London

Davenport, T H and Pearlson, K (1998) Two cheers for the virtual office, *MIT Sloan Management Review*, sloanreview.mit.edu/article/two-cheers-for-the-virtual-office/ (archived at https://perma.cc/77VU-ZJR8)

Dyer, C and Shepherd, K (2021) *Remote Work*, Kogan Page, London

Olson, M H (1983) Remote office work: Changing work patterns in space and time, 15 Communications of the ACM, 26(3), doi.org/10.1145/358061.358068 (archived at https://perma.cc/9YGR-ZJ8P)

Motivation

Pink, D H (2010) *Drive: The surprising truth about what motivates us*, Canongate Books, Edinburgh

Well-being

For information and research on boundary management, see the work of Ellen Kossek.

Trust

Covey, S M R and Merrill, R R (2008) *The Speed of Trust*, Simon and Schuster, London

Personal brand, presence and influence

Brummit, S (2020) *Remote Presence: A practical guide to communicating effectively in a remote environment*, FastPrint Publishing, Orton Southgate, UK

Cialdini, R (2006) *Influence: The psychology of persuasion*, Harper Business, New York

Dhawan, E (2021) *Digital Body Language: How to build trust and connection, no matter the distance*, St Martin's Press/Macmillan, New York

Peters, T (1997) The brand called you, *Fortune*, www.fastcompany.com/28905/brand-called-you (archived at https://perma.cc/M4RP-4JLS)

Schawbel, D (2009) *Me 2.0: Build a powerful brand to achieve career success*, Kaplan Trade, Manchester, UK

Hybrid work

Gajendran, R S and Harrison, D A (2007) The good, the bad and the unknown about telecommuting: Meta-analysis of psychological mediators and individual consequences, *Journal of Applied Psychology*, 92(6), 1524–541

Networking

Granovetter, M S (1973) The strength of weak ties: A network theory revisited, *American Journal of Sociology*, 78, 1360–380, doi.org/10.1007/978-3-658-21742-6_55 (archived at https://perma.cc/W2DM-JBNU)

Communication

Dennis, A, Valacich, J and Fuller, M (2008) Media, tasks and communication processes: A theory of media synchronicity, *MIS Quarterly*, www.researchgate.net/publication/220259966_Media_Tasks_and_Communication_Processes_A_Theory_of_Media_Synchronicity (archived at https://perma.cc/K6S5-7HHV)

Ramachandran, V (2021) Stanford researchers identify four causes for 'Zoom fatigue' and their simple fixes, Stanford News, news.stanford.edu/2021/02/23/four-causes-zoom-fatigue-solutions/ (archived at https://perma.cc/VKS9-MG7Q)

Effective meetings

Kline, N (1999) *Time to Think: Listening to ignite the human mind*, Cassell Illustrated, London

All the books in the Creating Success series

KoganPage